Internet

VISUAL™
Quick Tips

by Kate Shoup

Wiley Publishing, Inc.

Internet Visual™ Quick Tips

Published by
Wiley Publishing, Inc.
10475 Crosspoint Boulevard
Indianapolis, IN 46256

Published simultaneously in Canada

Copyright © 2008 by Wiley Publishing, Inc., Indianapolis, Indiana

Library of Congress Control Number: 2008929978

ISBN: 978-0-470-37344-6

Manufactured in the United States of America

10 9 8 7 6 5 4 3 2 1

Trademark Acknowledgments

Contact Us

For general information on our other products and services contact our Customer Care Department within the U.S. at 800-762-2974, outside the U.S. at 317-572-3993, or fax 317-572-4002.

For technical support please visit www.wiley.com/techsupport.

WILEY

Wiley Publishing, Inc.

Sales

Contact Wiley
at (800) 762-2974 or
fax (317) 572-4002.

Praise for Visual Books

"I have to praise you and your company on the fine products you turn out. I have twelve Visual books in my house. They were instrumental in helping me pass a difficult computer course. Thank you for creating books that are easy to follow. Keep turning out those quality books."

Gordon Justin (Brielle, NJ)

"What fantastic teaching books you have produced! Congratulations to you and your staff. You deserve the Nobel prize in Education. Thanks for helping me understand computers."

Bruno Tonon (Melbourne, Australia)

"A Picture Is Worth A Thousand Words! If your learning method is by observing or hands-on training, this is the book for you!"

Lorri Pegan-Durastante (Wickliffe, OH)

"Over time, I have bought a number of your 'Read Less - Learn More' books. For me, they are THE way to learn anything easily. I learn easiest using your method of teaching."

José A. Mazón (Cuba, NY)

"You've got a fan for life!! Thanks so much!!"

Kevin P. Quinn (Oakland, CA)

"I have several books from the Visual series and have always found them to be valuable resources."

Stephen P. Miller (Ballston Spa, NY)

"I have several of your Visual books and they are the best I have ever used."

Stanley Clark (Crawfordville, FL)

"Like a lot of other people, I understand things best when I see them visually. Your books really make learning easy and life more fun."

John T. Frey (Cadillac, MI)

"I have quite a few of your Visual books and have been very pleased with all of them. I love the way the lessons are presented!"

Mary Jane Newman (Yorba Linda, CA)

"Thank you, thank you, thank you...for making it so easy for me to break into this high-tech world."

Gay O'Donnell (Calgary, Alberta,Canada)

"I write to extend my thanks and appreciation for your books. They are clear, easy to follow, and straight to the point. Keep up the good work! I bought several of your books and they are just right! No regrets! I will always buy your books because they are the best."

Seward Kollie (Dakar, Senegal)

"I would like to take this time to thank you and your company for producing great and easy-to-learn products. I bought two of your books from a local bookstore, and it was the best investment I've ever made! Thank you for thinking of us ordinary people."

Jeff Eastman (West Des Moines, IA)

"Compliments to the chef!! Your books are extraordinary! Or, simply put, extra-ordinary, meaning way above the rest! THANKYOU THANKYOU THANKYOU! I buy them for friends, family, and colleagues."

Christine J. Manfrin (Castle Rock, CO)

Credits

Project Editor
Sarah Hellert

Sr. Acquisitions Editor
Jody Lefevere

Copy Editor
Scott Tullis

Technical Editor
Vince Averello

Editorial Manager
Robyn Siesky

Business Manager
Amy Knies

Sr. Marketing Manager
Sandy Smith

Editorial Assistant
Laura Sinise

Manufacturing
Allan Conley
Linda Cook
Paul Gilchrist
Jennifer Guynn

Book Design
Kathie Rickard

Production Coordinator
Erin Smith

Layout
Andrea Hornberger
Jennifer Mayberry

Screen Artist
Jill A. Proll

Cover Design
Mike Trent

Proofreader
Cindy Ballew

Quality Control
Jessica Kramer

Indexer
Broccoli Information Management

Vice President and Executive Group Publisher
Richard Swadley

Vice President and Publisher
Barry Pruett

Composition Director
Debbie Stailey

About the Author

During the course of her career as a freelance writer, **Kate Shoup** has written or co-written several books on various topics, including *Look & Learn FrontPage 2002*, *What Can You Do with a Major in Business*, *Not Your Mama's Beading*, *Not Your Mama's Stitching*, *Windows Vista Visual Encyclopedia*, and *Webster's New World English Grammar Handbook*. She has also co-written a screenplay, and worked as the Sports Editor for *NUVO Newsweekly*. Prior to striking out on her own, Kate worked as an editor at a computer-publishing company, where she engaged in such diverse professional activities as consulting on the development of new series, consulting on ways to improve the publishing workflow, and editing numerous standout titles. When not writing, Kate loves to ski (she was once nationally ranked), make jewelry, and play video poker — and she plays a mean game of 9-ball. Kate lives in Indianapolis, Indiana, with her daughter.

Author's Acknowledgments

The publication of any book is an enormous undertaking, involving many people, and this one is no exception. Thanks are due to Jody Lefevere for providing me with the opportunity to write this book, to Sarah Hellert for her expert guidance during the writing process, to Vince Averello for his technical expertise, and to Scott Tullis for catching my numerous grammatical slip-ups. Thanks, too, to the book's graphics team — Jill Proll, Mike Trent, and Tobin Wilkinson. Thanks to the book's production team, composed of Andrea Hornberger, Jennifer Mayberry, Erin Smith, Cindy Ballew, Jessica Kramer, and Broccoli Information Management. Finally, thanks to my family (especially my daughter Heidi) and friends — you know who you are.

How To Use This Book

Internet Visua Quick Tips includes tasks that reveal cool secrets, teach timesaving tricks, and explain great tips guaranteed to make you more productive with the Internet. The easy-to-use layout lets you work through all the tasks from beginning to end or jump in at random.

Who Is This Book For?

If you want to know the basics about the Internet, or if you want to learn shortcuts, tricks, and tips that let you work smarter and faster, this book is for you. And because you learn more easily when someone *shows* you how, this is the book for you.

Conventions Used In This Book

❶ Introduction
The introduction is designed to get you up to speed on the topic at hand.

❷ Steps
This book uses step-by-step instructions to guide you easily through each task. Numbered callouts on every screen shot show you exactly how to perform each task, step by step.

❸ Tips
Practical tips provide insights to save you time and trouble, caution you about hazards to avoid, and reveal how to do things with the Internet that you never thought possible!

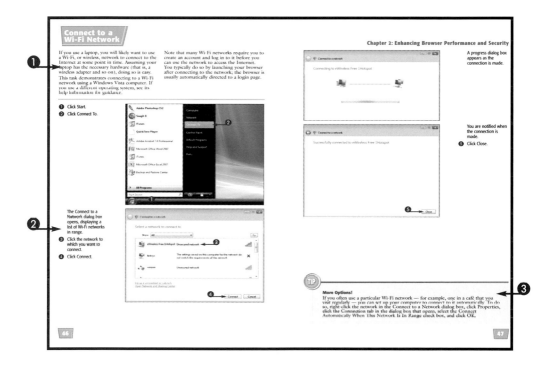

Table of Contents

chapter 4 Entering the Blogosphere

chapter 5 Managing and Sharing Photos Online

Chapter

1

Customizing Your Browser

A *Web browser* is a computer program that enables you to access and view Web pages. Popular Web browsers include Netscape Navigator, Opera, Firefox, Safari, and Internet Explorer (covered here). You launch your Web browser like you do any other program on your system — for example, from the Start menu (PC) or the Finder (Mac).

Although browsers do have their differences, they are fundamentally similar: You type the uniform resource locator (URL), or Web address, of the site you want to visit in the address bar, click the Back and Forward buttons to return to previous pages and then back again, and so on.

You can, however, adjust settings for your Web browser to direct how it looks and behaves. For example, you can reconfigure your browser's toolbars, specify which page loads at startup, control the size of the text that your browser displays, and even browse in full screen mode. Some browsers, including Internet Explorer 7, also offer *tabbed browsing*, which enables users to open multiple sites in a single browser window.

Before you adjust a setting, note its original state. That way, if you do not like the result of the adjustment, you can change it back.

Quick Tips

Set a Default Home Page

Chances are you frequently visit a particular Web site — for example, a news or weather site, an Internet e-mail site, or the home page for a search engine that you use on a regular basis.

If you want, you can set up your Web browser to automatically load that site whenever you launch the browser or click the browser's Home button. This saves you the trouble of

typing the site's uniform resource locator (URL), or Web address, or selecting the site from your Favorites.

Be aware that if a site has lots of graphics or other high-bandwidth content, it might not make the best default page for your browser because the site may require extra time to load.

---

1 With the page you want to set as the default open in your browser, click Tools.

Note: If the Tools button is not visible, click the toolbar options button (⬚) in the upper-right corner of the browser window; a list of additional buttons, including the Tools button, appears.

2 Click Internet Options.

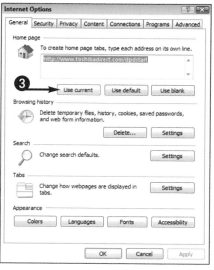

The Internet Options dialog box opens, displaying the General tab.

③ Click Use Current.

The URL listed in the Home Page text box changes to match the URL of the current page.

④ Click OK.

The Internet Options dialog box closes, and the page you indicated is set as the default.

Remove It!

If you no longer want to use the page you set as the browser's default home page, revert to the one your computer's manufacturer established by clicking Tools, clicking Internet Options, clicking Use Default, and clicking OK. Alternatively, you can configure your browser to display no page upon launch in order to speed up the startup process. To do so, click Use Blank in the Internet Options dialog box.

With literally billions of Web pages available online, the Internet is unquestionably an incredible resource for information. Its sheer scope, however, also makes it very difficult to search and sort. That means when you *do* find a site that you know you will revisit, you will probably want to use your browser to mark it as a favorite.

The uniform resource locator (URL), or Web address, for a site marked as a favorite is saved in a special list in your browser, called the Favorites Center. When you are ready to revisit the site, you can simply click the link to the site in the list.

You can organize your favorites by placing them in special folders, which you can create.

1 With the page you want to save as a favorite open in your browser, click the Add to Favorites button.

2 Click Add to Favorites.

The Add a Favorite dialog box opens.

3 Optionally, type a more descriptive name for the page.

● To save the page in a different folder, click the Create In ▾ and choose the desired folder.

● Alternatively, create a new folder by clicking New Folder, typing a name for the folder in the dialog box that appears, and clicking Create.

4 Click Add.

The page is added to your favorites.

When you save a page as a favorite, its uniform resource locator (URL), or Web address, is saved in a special list in Internet Explorer, called the Favorites Center. When you are ready to revisit the site, you can simply click the link to the site in the Favorites Center instead of, for example, using a search engine such as Google to locate the site again.

By default, sites in your Favorites Center are saved in the top-level Favorites folder. You can, however, create subfolders for storing the links to your favorite sites. This makes it easier to locate the page you want in your favorites. For more information about organizing your favorites in this way, see the task "Organize Your Favorites."

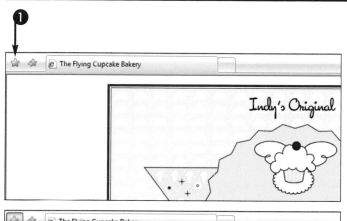

1 To view your list of favorites, click the Favorites Center button.

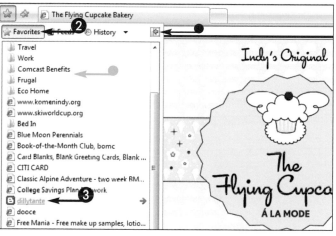

The Favorites Center opens.

2 If necessary, click Favorites.

A list of sites marked as favorites appears.

● If the link to the site you want to visit has been saved in a subfolder, click the folder.

3 Click the site you want to visit.

The site opens in your browser, and the Favorites Center closes.

● To prevent the Favorites Center from closing, click 📌 *before* you click the site you want to visit (📌 changes to ✕); click ✕ to close the Favorites Center.

Organize Your Favorites

By default, sites marked as favorites are saved in the top-level Favorites folder. This is fine if you have added only a few sites to your list of favorites. If, however, you add new sites on a regular basis, locating the site you want in your ever-growing list can become challenging.

To rectify this, you can organize your favorites by reordering them in your list, or by grouping related sites into subfolders. For

example, you might create one subfolder for news sites, a second subfolder for sites that relate to a favorite hobby, a third subfolder for travel sites, and so on.

Periodic pruning of your favorites list is another way to keep things organized. If you determine that you no longer want to include a site in your list of favorites, you can easily remove it.

CREATE A SUBFOLDER

1 Click the Add to Favorites button.

2 Click Organize Favorites.

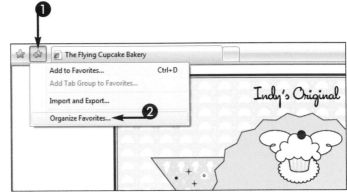

The Organize Favorites dialog box opens.

3 Click New Folder.

● A new folder appears at the bottom of the favorites list.

4 Type a name for the new folder and press Enter.

The new folder is renamed.

5 Click Close.

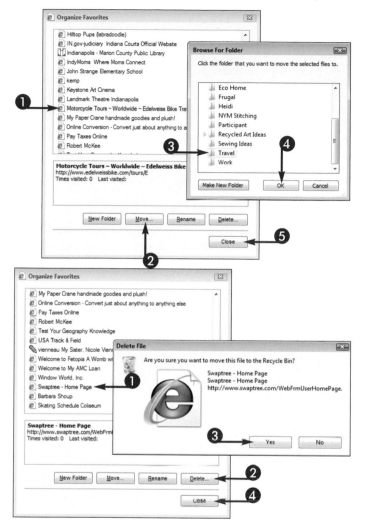

MOVE A FAVORITE TO A SUBFOLDER

① In the Organize Favorites dialog box, click the favorite you want to move.

Note: *To open the Organize Favorites dialog box, click the Add to Favorites button (⊡) and click Organize Favorites.*

② Click Move.

The Browse For Folder dialog box opens.

③ Click the subfolder into which you want to move the favorite.

④ Click OK.

⑤ Click Close.

DELETE A FAVORITE

① In the Organize Favorites dialog box, click the favorite you want to delete.

Note: *To open the Organize Favorites dialog box, click the Add to Favorites button (⊡) and click Organize Favorites.*

② Click Delete.

Your browser asks you to confirm the deletion.

③ Click Yes.

The site is deleted from your favorites.

④ Click Close.

More Options!

To change the order of a favorite in the Favorites Center, click the Favorites Center button (⊡) to open the Favorites Center, click Favorites if necessary, and click the favorite you want to move in the list and drag upward or downward. A line appears, indicating where the favorite will be moved in the list; release your mouse button when the line is in the desired spot.

View Your History List

Suppose you want to revisit a page you recently accessed, but you failed to save it as a favorite. Instead of using a search engine to locate the page again — a process that could be time consuming and frustrating — you can simply view your History list to locate the page.

To expedite this process, you can sort your History list in one of four ways: By Date, By Site, By Most Visited, or By Order Visited Today.

Note that you can change the number of days that your browser saves and displays in the History list. To do so, click Tools, click Internet Options, and click Settings in the Browsing History area of the General tab; then adjust the Days to Keep Pages in History setting.

① Click the Favorites Center button.

The Favorites Center opens.

② Click the down arrow (▾) next to the History button.

③ Choose the desired sort method — in this case, By Date.

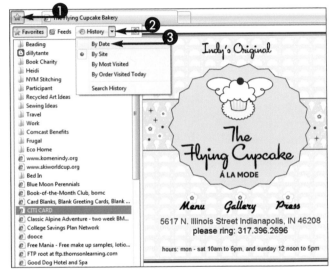

④ Click the day on which you visited the site in question.

A list of sites you visited on that day appears.

⑤ Click the desired site.

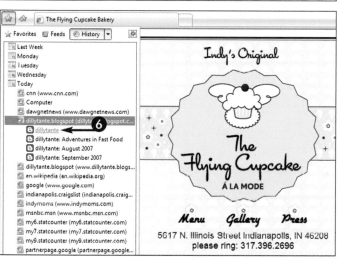

A list of pages you accessed on that site appears.

⑥ Click the desired page.

The page will open in your browser window.

More Options!

Another way to locate a page from your History list is to search for it. To do so, click the Favorites Center button (⭐), click the down arrow (▾) next to the History button, and choose Search History from the menu that appears. Type a relevant keyword in the Search For text box and click Search Now. Finally, click the desired page in the list of results that appears.

Customize Your Browser Toolbar

Your Web browser has a toolbar that provides buttons for moving backward and forward through pages you have visited, stopping a page from loading, refreshing a page, printing a page, and more. You can customize the toolbar by adding or removing buttons, rearranging the buttons, and so on. You can also switch to Full Screen mode, hiding the toolbar to provide more room to display Web pages. (In addition, you can hide or display the browser's menu bar, which offers alternative methods for navigating your browser and the Web in general.)

Once you have your toolbar set up just right, you can lock it in place to prevent accidental changes.

---

1 Click Tools.

Note: *If the Tools button is not visible, click the toolbar options button (⟩⟩) in the upper-right corner of the browser window; a list of additional buttons, including the Tools button, appears.*

2 Click Toolbars.

3 Click Customize.

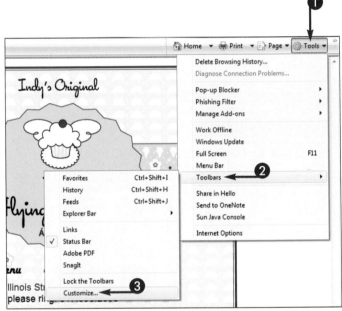

The Customize Toolbar dialog box opens.

4 In the Available Toolbar Buttons list, click a button you want to add to your toolbar – in this case, Full Screen.

5 Click Add.

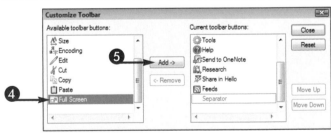

Indy's Original

Menu Gallery Press

5617 N. Illinois Street Indianapolis, IN 46208
please ring: 317.396.2696

hours: mon - sat 10am to 6pm. and sunday 12 noon to 5pm

● The selected button appears in the Current Toolbar Buttons list.

6 To change the order in which the button appears on the toolbar, click it in the Current Toolbar Buttons list.

7 Click Move Up or Move Down as many times as necessary to situate the button as desired.

Note: To remove a button, click it in the Current Toolbar Buttons list and click Remove.

● The button's order in the list changes.

● Depending on where in the list the button has been moved, it may appear on the toolbar.

● If the button does not appear on the toolbar, click the toolbar options button to access it.

8 Click Close.

Note: To lock the toolbar buttons in place, click the Tools button, click Toolbars, and click Lock the Toolbars.

TIP

More Options!
In addition to customizing your browser's toolbar, you can also specify whether the Internet Explorer menu bar should be shown. To do so, right-click the toolbar and choose Menu Bar to check or uncheck that option in the menu that appears. The Internet Explorer menu bar simply offers an additional set of options by which you can access various browser tools and commands.

Add an Address Bar to Your Windows Taskbar

When most users want to visit a Web site, they typically launch their Web browsers first and then type the Web address for the page they want to visit in their browser window's address bar. You can, however, save yourself a step by adding an address bar to your Windows taskbar — the space along the bottom of your screen that contains the Start button, buttons for currently running programs, the notification area, and other handy tools. Then, anytime you want to visit a Web site, you can simply type its address in the taskbar's address bar; Windows automatically launches your browser and opens the page you specified.

---

① Right-click a blank area of the Windows taskbar.

A menu appears.

② Click Toolbars.

A submenu appears.

③ Click Address.

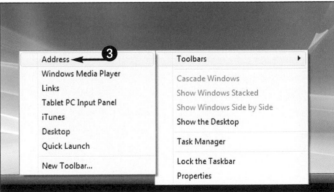

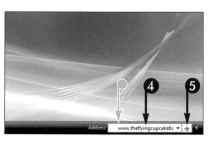

- An address bar appears.

4 Type the URL for the page you want to visit.

5 Click the arrow or press Enter.

Windows launches your browser and opens the page whose address you typed.

More Options!

As you type the desired Web address in the Windows taskbar's address bar, a list of addresses that match the text you have typed thus far appears. If the address you seek is in the list, you can click it there instead of typing it in full in the address bar. You can also access this list by clicking the address bar ⏷.

When your Web browser displays its toolbar, status bar, menu bar, and so on, its controls can occupy much of the space that it could use to display Web pages. To give a Web page more screen space, you can switch to full screen mode. In this mode, your browser hides various window controls, such as its title bar, status bar, and all toolbars (although it does leave the vertical scrollbar in place so you can move up and down the page). To again display the window controls, simply move your cursor to the top of the window; the controls slide into view.

❶ **Click Tools.**

Note: *If the Tools button is not visible, click the toolbar options button (⏷) in the upper-right corner of the browser window; a list of additional buttons, including the Tools button, appears.*

❷ **Click Full Screen.**

The page appears in full screen mode.

③ To again view the window controls, move your cursor to the top of the screen.

● The controls reappear.

④ To restore the window to regular view, click Tools.

⑤ Click Full Screen.

Note: *Another way to return the window to regular view is to click the Restore button (* *) in the upper-right corner of the screen.*

The window will revert to regular view.

TIP

More Options!

An even quicker way to view your pages in full screen mode is to press the F11 key on your keyboard. Click it again to revert back to regular mode. Other keyboard shortcuts, which apply in both full screen and regular mode, include pressing Alt+left arrow and/or Alt+right arrow to move backward and/or forward through pages you have already visited.

Increase or Decrease Text Size

Instead of indicating a specific size for text, most Web pages contain codes that specify the *relative* size of text. For example, the person who built the page might indicate that the Web page's title should be *larger* than the normal text that appears below it — but not the precise size. Your Web browser interprets these codes according to its own setting to determine exactly how the text appears. You can adjust this setting to control how large or small text appears on-screen.

This setting applies to text only; adjusting it will not affect how large or small graphics appear on your screen — even if the graphics contain words. In that case, you can use your browser's zoom tools to zoom in and out.

CHANGE THE TEXT SIZE SETTING

1 Click Page.

Note: *If the Page button is not visible, click the toolbar options button (□) in the upper-right corner of the browser window; a list of additional buttons, including the Page button, appears.*

2 Click Text Size.

3 Click a size option (here, Largest).

The text on the screen is resized.

Chapter 1: Customizing Your Browser

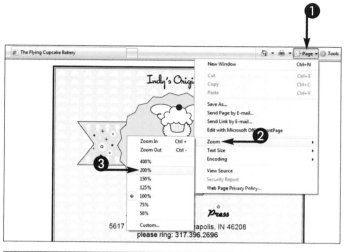

ZOOM IN

① Click Page.

Note: If the Page button is not visible, click the toolbar options button (📄) in the upper-right corner of the browser window; a list of additional buttons, including the Page button, appears.

② Click Zoom.

③ Click a zoom option (here, 200%).

The browser zooms in on (or out of, depending on your selection in Step 3) the page.

Note: An even faster way to zoom in on or out of a page is to press Ctrl++ (plus sign) or Ctrl+- (minus sign).

Did You Know?

Most Web pages are coded to use a particular font, but some are designed to display whatever font your browser uses by default. To change this default, click Tools and click Internet Options. In the Internet Options dialog box, click Fonts in the General tab, click the font you want to use in the Webpage Font and Plain Text Font lists, and click OK twice to close both dialog boxes.

Browse Multiple Pages with Quick Tabs

Suppose you are using the Internet to compare the price of flights offered on various airline Web sites. In earlier versions of Internet Explorer, you would have had to open a separate browser window for each site; switching from one open page to another was often cumbersome.

To rectify this, Microsoft developed a feature called Quick Tabs. With Quick Tabs, when you open multiple Web pages at once, each one appears in the same browser window in its own tab. To switch to a different Web page, you simply click the page's tab.

Quick Tabs also supports a special view, called Quick Tabs view. In it, all the pages that are open in your browser appear at once.

① To launch a page in a new tab, click the blank tab that appears to the right of any populated ones.

A blank page opens.

② Type a Web address in the address bar.

● The page you specified opens.

③ To switch to a different page, click its tab.

The page whose tab you clicked appears in the browser window.

④ To view multiple pages in Quick Tabs view, click the Quick Tabs button.

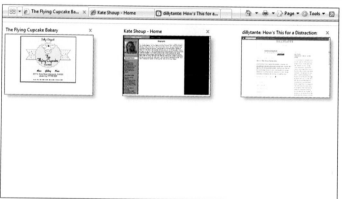

The open pages appear in Quick Tabs view.

Note: *Click any page in Quick Tabs view to view it in its regular display mode. Alternatively, close Quick Tabs view by again clicking the Quick Tabs button (**).*

TIP

Try This!

Another way to switch to a different page is to click the down arrow (▾) next to the Quick Tabs button (▦) and choose the desired page from the list that appears. To close a page, right-click its tab and click Close, or click the tab's Close button.

Chapter 2

Enhancing Browser Performance and Security

Chances are you typically use a high-speed connection to access the Internet. Even so, you can take certain steps to enhance your Internet experience. For example, you can use Windows Defender to scan for and eliminate spyware, which is known to slow your system. You can also adjust Internet Explorer's Pop-up Blocker utility to prevent annoying pop-up ads from consuming system resources.

In addition to taking steps to speed up your system, you can also change settings to boost system security. For example, using Internet Explorer's Phishing Filter enables you to ward off phishers who seek to obtain your personal information. Also available are browser settings that enable you to disable cookies and delete your browsing history. You can also change your browser's general security settings to better protect your system. In addition to changing browser settings, you can also set up Windows Firewall to protect your system from outside threats. Note that in addition to all this, you should also install and run antivirus software to prevent viruses and worms from infiltrating your computer.

Finally, this chapter outlines how to prevent users from viewing objectionable content, and how to connect to a Wi-Fi network.

Quick Tips

Test Your Internet Connection Speed

Most Internet service providers advertise the top speed of their service. In reality, however, your Internet connection might not be as speedy as promised. That is because Internet speeds can fluctuate depending on how many people are online. This is especially true of cable-based connections, which can vary greatly if many of your neighbors use the same service.

If you notice that your Internet connection seems particularly slow, you can test its speed using one of several Web sites that offer special speed-testing tools.

Typically, these tools work by both uploading and downloading a large file of a given size between the Web site and your computer and determining how long each operation takes.

---

① Type **http://us.mcafee.com/root/speedometer/default.asp** in your browser's address bar and press Enter.

The Internet Connection Speedometer page opens.

② Click the Click Here to Test Now link.

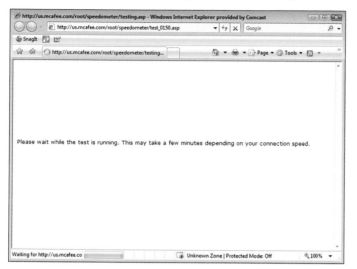

The Internet Connection Speedometer tests your connection speed.

● Results appear here.

More Options!

The site shown here is just one of several online resources for testing your connection speed. Others include www.dslreports.com/stest, www.pcpitstop.com/internet/default.asp, and bandwidthplace.com/speedtest.

Scan for Spyware with Windows Defender

Spyware is software that is installed on your computer, usually without your knowledge. It can deluge your system with pop-up ads, and it typically transmits data about your Web-surfing activities to a third party, such as a company seeking marketing data or a hacker with more sinister motives. Even if spyware is relatively benign, it can dramatically affect your computer's performance.

If you use Windows Vista, you can combat this with a utility called Windows Defender; it scans your system for spyware and uninstalls it if detected.

Windows Defender offers a real-time protection feature — enabled by default — to alert you if a spyware program attempts to install itself on your machine or if any program attempts to change your Windows settings without your knowledge.

① Click Start.

② Click Control Panel.

The Control Panel window opens.

③ Click Security.

The Security window opens.

④ Click here to scan for spyware and other potentially unwanted programs.

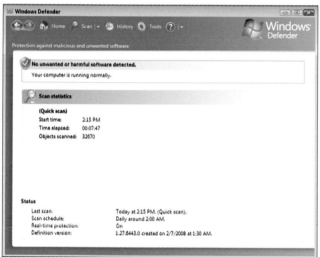

Note: *If you are prompted for an administrator password, type your password or click Allow.*

Windows Defender scans your computer and informs you of the results when the scan is complete.

More Options!

To configure Windows to automatically scan your system, click Tools in the Windows Defender window and click Options. Under Automatic Scanning, select Automatically Scan My Computer, then set the scan frequency, time of day, and scan type. If you want Windows to remove spyware it detects during a scan, select Apply Actions on Detected Items and, under Default Actions, choose Remove from each drop-down list. Finally, click Save.

Change Pop-Up Blocker Settings

Usually created by advertisers, a *pop-up* is a small browser window containing an advertisement that opens automatically when you visit a site. In addition to being annoying, pop-ups can negatively affect system performance.

Internet Explorer 7 features Pop-up Blocker, which is enabled by default. It prevents pop-ups from opening, instead displaying a

message in the information bar (near the top of the browser window) indicating that a pop-up has been blocked, and giving you the option of viewing it if desired.

If Pop-up Blocker consistently blocks a pop-up that you want to display when you visit a certain site, you can configure the utility to do so. You can also change the filter level to allow pop-ups from secure sites or to disallow all pop-ups.

---

① In the Internet Explorer window, click Tools.

② Click Pop-up Blocker.

● If you want to turn off Pop-up Blocker completely (not recommended), select this option.

③ Click Pop-up Blocker Settings.

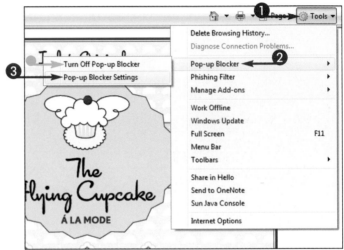

The Pop-up Blocker Settings dialog box opens.

④ To allow pop-ups for a particular site, type the site's Web address.

⑤ Click Add.

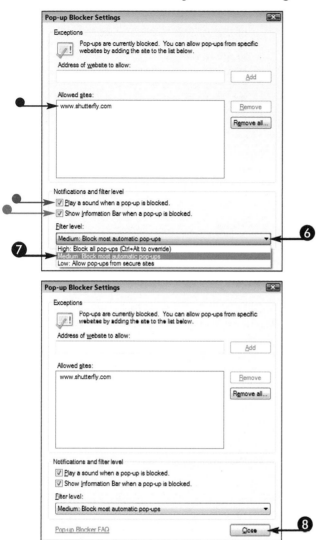

● The Web address you typed appears in the Allowed Sites list.

● Select this check box if you want your computer to play a sound when a pop-up is blocked.

● Select this check box if you want to see a notification in the information bar when a pop-up is blocked.

⑥ Click the Filter Level ▾.

⑦ Select the desired filter level.

⑧ Click Close.

Internet Explorer applies the Pop-up Blocker settings you chose.

More Options!

By default, pop-ups appear in separate windows. You can, however, configure your system to display pop-ups in tabs. To do so, click Tools and click Internet Options. In the Internet Options dialog box that opens, click the General tab and, under Tabs, click Settings. The Tabbed Browsing Settings dialog box opens; click Always Open Pop-ups in a New Tab, and then click OK in both dialog boxes to close them.

Detect Phishing Web Sites

Phishing (pronounced *fishing*) is an attempt by a malicious party to obtain private information from an unsuspecting computer user. It typically involves an e-mail message that appears to be from a legitimate source, such as a bank informing the user that his or her account information must be updated and directing the user to click a link to access a Web site where he or she can enter the

necessary information. This link does not direct the user to the trusted source's Web site, however. Instead, it directs the user to a site that mimics the trusted site in order to steal personal information. Internet Explorer's Phishing Filter helps detect these fraudulent Web sites and helps users from falling prey to fraudulent activity.

ENABLE AUTOMATIC SITE CHECKING

① In the Internet Explorer window, click Tools.

② Click Phishing Filter.

③ Click Turn On Automatic Website Checking.

Note: *You can direct Internet Explorer to check whether the current Web site is a phishing site by selecting Check This Website.*

④ Click Turn On Automatic Phishing Filter.

⑤ Click OK.

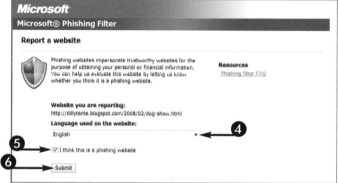

REPORT A FRAUDULENT WEB SITE

① With the site you want to report open in your browser, click Tools.

② Click Phishing Filter.

③ Click Report This Web Site.

A Microsoft Web page opens.

④ Choose the language used on the suspect Web site.

⑤ Select the I Think This Is a Phishing Website check box.

⑥ Click Submit.

Note: *You can also follow these steps to notify Microsoft that a site they have flagged as fraudulent is in fact trustworthy.*

Attention!

Regularly review your financial statements. If you discover you have been a victim of fraud, file a report with the local police, change the passwords or PINs on all of your online accounts, contact your bank and credit card issuers, and place a fraud alert on your credit reports (your bank or financial advisor can tell you how). Finally, if you are aware of any accounts that were opened fraudulently, close them.

Change Internet Explorer Security Settings

Not all Web sites are created equal. Some are trustworthy, with practices and policies in place to protect visitors. Others are sketchy at best.

For this reason, Internet Explorer assigns all Web sites to one of four *security zones*: Internet, Local Intranet, Trusted Sites, and Restricted Sites. The level of security applied to a site depends on the zone to which that site is assigned.

The default security level for sites in the Internet zone is Medium High. The default security level for sites in the Local Intranet, Trusted Sites, and Restricted Sites zones are Medium Low, Medium, and High, respectively.

If Microsoft has assigned a particular Web site to a zone that is too restrictive (or not restrictive enough), you can change zones.

ADD A SITE TO A SECURITY ZONE

① With the site whose zone you want to change open in Internet Explorer, click the Tools button.

Note: *You can tell which zone you are in by checking the bottom-right corner of your Internet Explorer Web browser window, in the status bar.*

② Click Internet Options.

The Internet Options dialog box opens.

③ Click the Security tab.

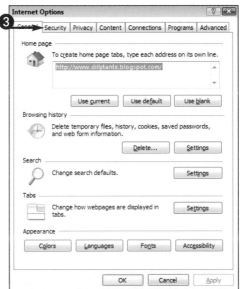

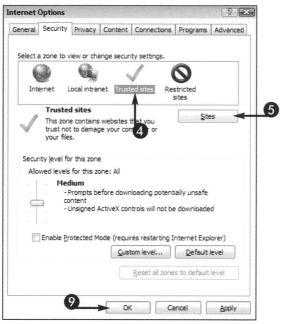

④ Click a security zone (here, Trusted Sites) to apply it to the site.

⑤ Click the Sites button.

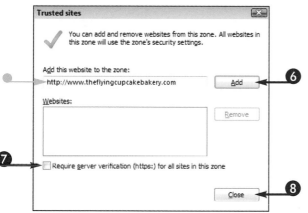

● The Trusted Sites dialog box opens, with the Web site listed under Add This Website to the Zone.

⑥ Click Add.

⑦ If the site is not a secure site, deselect the Require Server Verification (HTTPS:) for All Sites in This Zone check box.

⑧ Click Close to close the Trusted Sites dialog box.

⑨ Click OK to close the Internet Options dialog box.

Remove It!

Just as you can add a site to a security zone, so, too, can you remove one. When you do, the site reverts back to the default Internet zone. To remove a site from a zone, click the security zone of the site you want to remove in the Internet Options dialog box's Security tab, click Sites, click the site you want to remove, and click Remove.

Change Internet Explorer
Security Settings *(continued)*

Each of the four security zones has a recommended level of security applied to it. As mentioned, the Internet zone's default level is Medium High, the Local Intranet zone's is Medium Low, the Trusted Sites zone's is Medium, and the Restricted Sites zone's is High. (*Default level* refers to the security level that Microsoft recommends for a zone.)

You can modify the security level for the Internet, Local Intranet, and Trusted Sites zones to either increase or reduce the level of protection needed. For example, if you experience problems loading a particular page, then you may need to reduce the security level, at least temporarily, to view the page normally. (Note that you cannot change the Restricted Sites zone's security level.)

**CUSTOMIZE THE
SECURITY LEVEL OF
A SECURITY ZONE**

① Click the Tools button.

② Click Internet Options.

The Internet Options dialog box opens.

③ Click the Security tab.

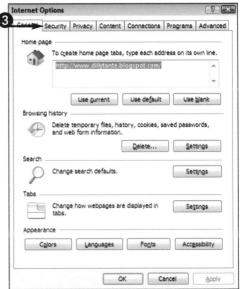

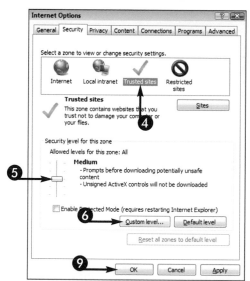

④ Click a security zone.

⑤ Adjust the slider under Security Level for This Zone to change the security level.

⑥ To further customize the security settings for the selected zone, click Custom Level.

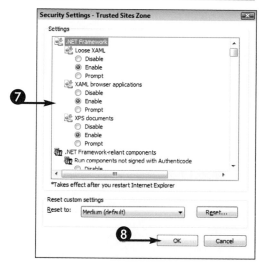

The zone's Security Settings dialog box opens.

⑦ Adjust each individual setting as desired.

⑧ Click OK to close the Security Settings dialog box.

⑨ Click OK to close the Internet Options dialog box.

Remove It!

To return the custom settings to their default, recommended levels, open the Internet Options dialog box, click the Security tab, click the zone whose settings you want to change, click the Default Level button, and click OK.

Internet Explorer 7 saves bits of information (called *cookies*) to your hard drive when you visit certain sites on the Internet. For example, it might save the user name you typed to access an account you hold with a site to save you the trouble of typing this information on your next visit.

The browser also keeps a list, called the History list, of the sites you visit during a browsing session. Especially if you are using a public computer, as in an Internet café or a public library, you should delete your browsing history — that is, your History list, any cookies, and so on — when you finish your session. (Note that you should always close the browser when you are done using it.)

---

1 Click Tools.

2 Click Delete Browsing History.

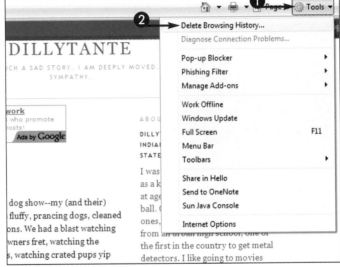

The Delete Browsing History dialog box opens.

3 Click Delete All.

Note: *In addition to removing cookies and your History list, clicking Delete All also deletes temporary Internet files (used to speed up the loading of sites you have visited before), as well as any form data and passwords you have entered.*

Internet Explorer asks
you to confirm the
deletion.

④ Click Yes.

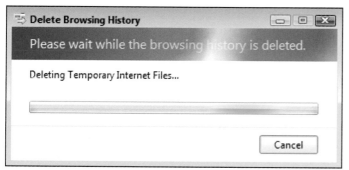

A progress dialog box
appears, indicating
the status of the
deletion, and the
Delete Browsing
History dialog box
closes.

More Options!
If you want to delete your History list but not, for example, your cookies, you can
easily do so. Simply launch the Delete Browsing History dialog box as outlined in
this task, and then click the Delete button for the category of information you want
to erase. Click Yes when prompted to confirm and, when the deletion is complete,
click Close.

A *cookie* is a tiny data file transmitted to your browser by a Web server and vice versa. It might contain information such as your login data, preferences, and the like.

Although most cookies are designed to make your browsing experience more pleasant by storing information you enter on a Web site, some, such as those created when you click

banner ads, can compromise your privacy by tracking the sites you visit.

If you are concerned about the use of cookies on your system, you can block them either across the board or on a case-by-case basis. One approach is to begin by blocking all cookies, and then allow certain ones from trustworthy sites as needed.

① Click Tools.

② Click Internet Options.

The Internet Options dialog box opens.

③ Click the Privacy tab.

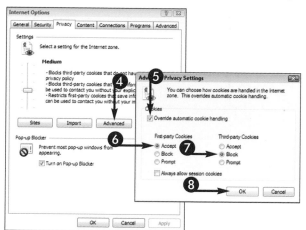

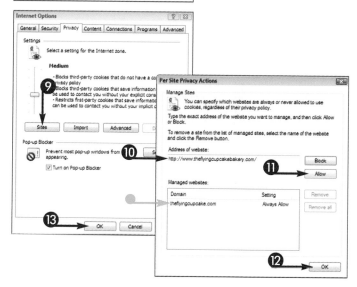

④ Click Advanced.

The Advanced Privacy Settings dialog box opens.

⑤ Select the Override Automatic Cookie Handling check box.

⑥ Indicate how you want to handle first-party cookies.

⑦ Indicate how you want to handle third-party cookies.

⑧ Click OK.

⑨ Click Sites.

The Per Site Privacy Actions dialog box opens.

⑩ Type the Web address of a site for which you want to block or allow cookies.

⑪ Click Block or Allow.

● The site appears in the Managed Websites list.

⑫ Click OK to close the Per Site Privacy Actions dialog box.

⑬ Click OK to close the Internet Options dialog box.

More Options!

Cookies come in two varieties: temporary, which are removed from your computer after you close your browser, and persistent, which remain on your computer even after you close your browser. These varieties are both further categorized into first-party cookies, which come from the Web site you are currently viewing, and third-party cookies, which come from advertisements on a site, such as banner ads.

Configure Windows Firewall

When you enable and configure Windows Firewall, available with Windows Vista, you set up a layer of protection to shield your computer or network from intrusion that can put your system at risk. A *firewall* creates a barrier between your system and a network such as the Internet.

System intrusion can take many forms. One example is an *Internet worm* — a type of computer virus that can, among other things,

leave behind files that create an opening for others who want to access your computer or steal your passwords.

Windows Firewall monitors all programs that access the Internet from your computer or try to communicate with you from an external source, automatically acting to block certain programs that may compromise the security of your system.

ENABLE WINDOWS FIREWALL

① In the Control Panel window, click Security.

Note: To open the Control Panel window, click Start and click Control Panel.

The Security window opens.

② Click Turn Windows Firewall On or Off.

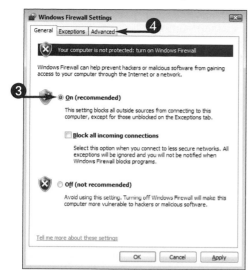

The Windows Firewall dialog box appears, displaying the General tab.

③ Click On.

④ Click the Advanced tab.

⑤ Click to deselect any connection setting for which you do not want to enable the firewall.

⑥ Click OK.

Windows Firewall is configured and enabled.

Important!

Just because you use the Windows Firewall does not mean that you do not need other forms of protection, including common-sense measures that limit your risk of exposure to threats. For example, you should be careful when opening e-mail attachments or other files from any source, even a trusted one. Even more importantly, you should run antivirus software such as that offered by McAfee.

You can control whether Windows Firewall blocks certain programs or connections from accessing your system or the Internet. An *exception* is a program or connection that you want to allow so that it does not limit your ability to work or communicate. Managing these exceptions is vital so that the firewall does not block your critical network communications.

For example, when you instant-message with someone, you often create a short-term connection between your systems. The firewall may block this connection unless you identify the connection as okay. You can do this by configuring the firewall ahead of time or when you receive a message from the firewall, asking if you want to block or unblock a connection or program.

MANAGE EXCEPTIONS

❶ In the Control Panel window, click Security.

Note: To open the Control Panel window, click Start and click Control Panel.

The Security window opens.

❷ Click Allow a Program through Windows Firewall.

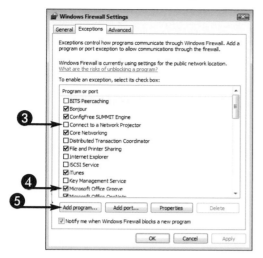

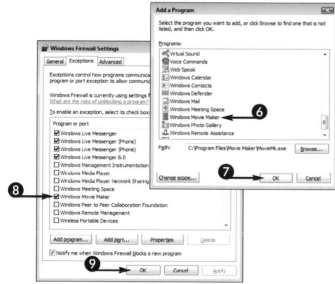

The Windows Firewall
Settings dialog box
appears, displaying
the Exceptions tab.

③ To unblock a program,
select the check box
next to the program's
name in the list.

④ To block a program,
deselect the check box
next to the program's
name in the list.

⑤ To block or unblock a
program that is not in
the list, click Add
Program.

The Add a Program
dialog box opens.

⑥ Click the program in
the list.

⑦ Click OK to close the
Add a Program dialog
box.

⑧ Select or deselect the
program's check box
in the Exceptions tab.

⑨ Click OK to close the
Windows Firewall
Settings dialog box.

Remove It!

If, after customizing your Windows Firewall configuration, you want it to operate as
it originally did, you can restore the default settings by clicking Restore Defaults in
the Windows Firewall dialog box's Advanced tab.

Although the Internet can be both educational and entertaining, it can also expose users to unwanted subject matter, such as sexually explicit or violent content. To restrict what types of Web sites and other Internet resources are available on your PC, you can enable Internet Explorer 7's Content Advisor tool. Content Advisor uses ratings that Web sites provide to block or allow certain content, depending on the settings you choose. (Web sites that are unrated are blocked by default.) You can also specify that specific Web sites be blocked or allowed. Only users with the password you set can override Content Advisor.

① In Internet Explorer 7's Internet Options dialog box, click the Content tab.

Note: To open Internet Explorer 7's Internet Options dialog box, click Tools and click Internet Options.

② Under Content Advisor, click Enable.

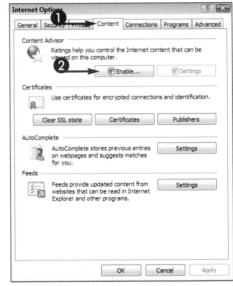

The Content Advisor dialog box opens.

③ In the Ratings tab, click a content category to view or adjust its rating level.

④ Drag the slider to change the rating level — that is, what content in the selected category users are allowed to see.

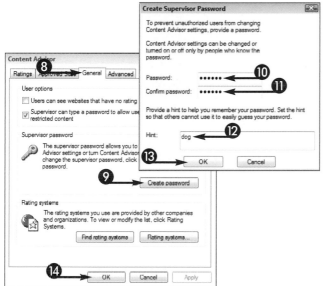

⑤ Click the Approved Sites tab.

⑥ Type the Web address for a site you want to always allow or always block.

⑦ Click Always or Never.

● The site is added to the list of allowed or blocked sites.

⑧ Click the General tab.

⑨ Click Create Password.

⑩ Type the password you want to use to override Content Advisor settings.

⑪ Retype the password.

⑫ Type a password hint.

⑬ Click OK to close the Create Supervisor Password dialog box.

⑭ Click OK to close the Content Advisor dialog box.

⑮ Click OK to close the Internet Options dialog box.

More Options!

To view information about the rating system Content Advisor uses, click the More Info button on the Content Advisor dialog box's Ratings tab. Internet Explorer launches the rating service's Web site, where you can read about the service's general philosophy, background, and so on.

Connect to a Wi-Fi Network

If you use a laptop, you will likely want to use a Wi-Fi, or wireless, network to connect to the Internet at some point in time. Assuming your laptop has the necessary hardware (that is, a wireless adapter and so on), doing so is easy.

This task demonstrates connecting to a Wi-Fi network using a Windows Vista computer. If you use a different operating system, see its help information for guidance.

Note that many Wi-Fi networks require you to create an account and log in to it before you can use the network to access the Internet. You typically do so by launching your browser after connecting to the network; the browser is usually automatically directed to a login page.

① Click Start.

② Click Connect To.

The Connect to a Network dialog box opens, displaying a list of Wi-Fi networks in range.

③ Click the network to which you want to connect.

④ Click Connect.

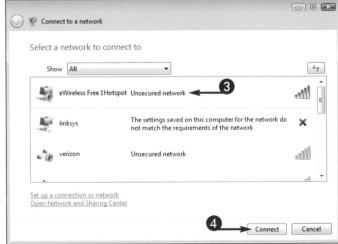

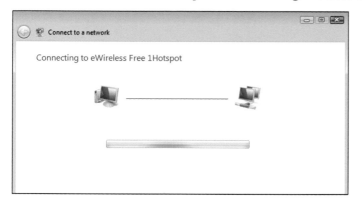

A progress dialog box appears as the connection is made.

Connecting to eWireless Free 1Hotspot

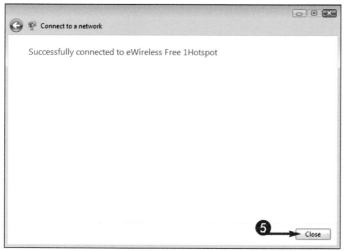

You are notified when the connection is made.

⑤ Click Close.

Successfully connected to eWireless Free 1Hotspot

More Options!

If you often use a particular Wi-Fi network — for example, one in a café that you visit regularly — you can set up your computer to connect to it automatically. To do so, right-click the network in the Connect to a Network dialog box, click Properties, click the Connection tab in the dialog box that opens, select the Connect Automatically When This Network Is In Range check box, and click OK.

Harnessing the Power of Google

Because it indexes literally billions of Web documents, Google is understandably the top search site on the Internet. Most users, however, harness only a fraction of Google's power because they limit themselves to running basic searches on the site. That is, they simply type a word or phrase in Google's main page and sift through the countless hits the site returns in the hopes of uncovering just the right link. A better approach is to use Google's advanced search tools and to set your search preferences to narrow your results to those that are most relevant.

In addition, users can exploit Google's many other offerings, such as its foreign language translation tools, image-search capabilities, Book Search feature, news aggregator, mapping functions, calendar software, and more. Moreover, the Google Toolbar, which you can install on your browser, provides access to many of Google's features — without even requiring you to launch Google's Web site in your browser window.

To assist you with its many tools, Google has established a thorough Help Center; to access it, click the More link, click Even More, and click the Help Center link along the bottom of the page.

Quick Tips

When you use Google's main Search page to locate a Web site, Google returns as many matching links as possible by default. Indeed, it may well return *millions* of links — far more than you can reasonably digest — and often with the one that you really need buried in the results.

To pare down these results to a more manageable set, you can use Google's

Advanced Search page. It enables you to limit results to pages that contain a particular phrase, that omit a certain word or phrase, that contain the word or phrase in a certain part of the page (such as the title), that are written in a certain language, that are created in a particular file format, and so on.

---

1 Type **www.google.com** in your browser's address bar and press Enter.

2 Click Advanced Search.

Google's Advanced Search page opens.

3 Enter words for which you want to search — as well as ones that should be omitted from the results — in the Find Results fields.

4 Click the down arrow (▼) and choose how many results you want displayed per page.

5 To limit results to pages that feature a particular language, click the Language ▼ and select the desired language.

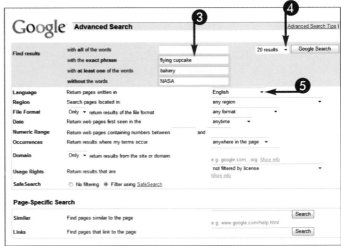

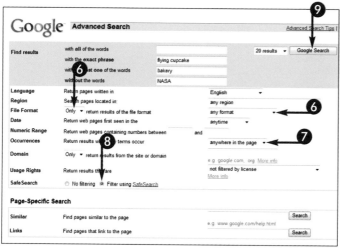

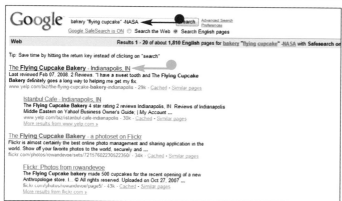

⑥ If the page you seek is of a particular type — say, PDF — use the File Format settings to limit results to this format.

⑦ Use the Occurrences setting to indicate where on the page the keywords should appear — for example, anywhere on the page, in its title, and so on.

⑧ To omit sites with adult content from your results, click Filter Using Safe Search.

⑨ Click Google Search.

● Google displays the results of your search, with links to pages that match your keyword entries.

● Notice the operators that appear in the Search box. The quotes around "Flying Cupcake" indicate that only pages with that exact phrase should appear in the results. The hyphen before "NASA" denotes that pages with that term should be omitted.

More Options!

In addition to the operators shown here, you can use other operators to refine your search. For example, typing ~ before a search term returns results that contain synonyms of the term. Another example is the * character, which acts as a *wildcard*. For example, typing an * between the words "flying" and "bakery" returns results with one or more words between the two words you typed.

By default, when you use Google to conduct a search, the site's results include all matching pages, regardless of language — although Google does use a moderate amount of filtering technology to screen out sites that contain potentially offensive content. Results are displayed in groups of ten per page, in the same browser window as the one you used to enter your search criteria.

If you want, you can change these behaviors by adjusting your Google preferences. For example, you can specify that only matching pages written in a particular language be displayed in your results, or that more stringent filtering technologies be applied to screen out all offensive content (or that less stringent filtering be applied to allow content).

① Type **www.google.com** in your browser's address bar and press Enter.

② Click Preferences.

The Preferences page opens.

③ Click the Interface Language ▾ and select the language you want Google to use in tips and messages to you.

④ To limit results to pages written in particular languages, click Search Only for Pages Written in These Languages.

⑤ Click the check box next to each desired language.

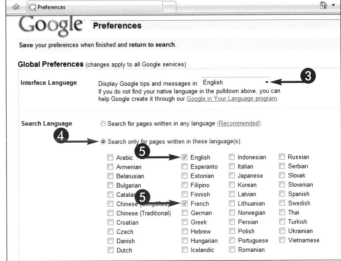

⑥ Adjust the filter level of Google's SafeSearch feature to allow or disallow pages with explicit content.

⑦ Click the Number of Results ▾ to change how many links appear on each results page.

● If you want links you click in the results to appear in a new browser window, select the Results Window check box.

⑧ Click Save Preferences.

A dialog box appears, confirming that your preferences have been saved.

⑨ Click OK.

More Options!

Google can save the preferences you enter only if cookies have been enabled on your Web browser. *Cookies* are tiny data files transmitted to your browser by a Web server and vice versa. For more information about managing cookies, refer to the task "Manage Cookies" in Chapter 2.

Unless you adjust your Google Preferences to display only pages written in a particular language, Google may well return pages written in other languages.

If you do not understand the language in which a particular page is written, Google may be able to translate the page for you. The translation may be clumsy, but will likely be adequate to convey the page's basic meaning to you. (Note that only text on the page can be translated; graphic images, even if they contain words, will remain in their original form.)

In addition to translating pages, Google offers other translation services on its Language Tools page. For example, you can use tools on this page to search across languages, and to translate text that you type.

TRANSLATE A PAGE

1 In your Google search results, click Translate This Page next to the link to a page you want translated.

Note: *In this example, Google searched French pages for the term entered. To instruct Google to search pages of a certain language, follow the steps in the preceding task.*

● Google translates the page.

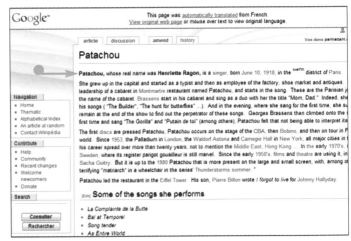

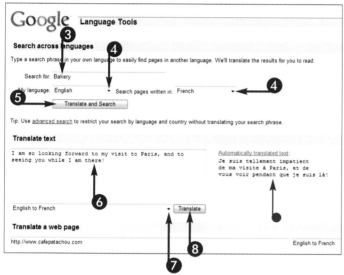

EXPLORE GOOGLE'S TRANSLATION TOOLS

① Type **www.google.com** in your browser's address bar and press Enter.

② Click Language Tools.

③ To search across languages, type a word or phrase in your language.

④ Specify your language, and the language in which you want to find sites containing your word or phrase.

⑤ Click Translate and Search.

Google returns a list of sites that match your criteria.

⑥ To translate text, type the text in your language.

⑦ Specify the language to which you want the text translated.

⑧ Click Translate.

● Google translates the text.

More Options!

The Google Language Tools page also enables you to translate a Web page by typing its Web address, visit your local Google site (that is, the one dedicated to your country), and change the language used on the Google interface. Note that if your language is not offered, you can help Google create a language-specific interface by becoming a volunteer translator.

If you frequently conduct Google searches, then the Google Toolbar is for you. It is a special toolbar that appears just under your browser's address bar. With it, you can bypass Google's Web site, typing your search parameters directly into the toolbar. In addition to enabling you to search, the Google Toolbar also includes features that enable you

to rank pages, highlight keywords in a document, and more. You can also quickly access Google's home page by clicking the Google button on the left side of the toolbar. This powerful tool is completely free, and you download and install it just as you would any other software.

---

① Type **http://toolbar.google.com** and press Enter.

② Click Install Google Toolbar and follow the on-screen instructions to download and install it.

● The Google Toolbar appears along the top of the screen.

③ To run a Google search from the toolbar, type a keyword or phrase.

④ Click Go.

A Google search results page opens.

⑤ Click a link to open the desired page.

The page opens.

⑥ Optionally, click the Highlight button.

● Each instance of the keyword or phrase you typed is highlighted in the Web page.

More Options!

Click the Google button ([G]) on the left side of the toolbar to display a menu containing links to various Google tools. You may also see a Manage option; clicking it launches a Toolbar Options dialog box that includes various customization settings. To uninstall the toolbar, click the Settings button on the right side of the toolbar, click Help, and click Uninstall.

With billions of images indexed, and more added every day, Google's Image Search is clearly the most comprehensive tool on the Web for locating images.

You can use many of the same search tools with Image Search as you can with Google's regular Web search. For example, you can use quotes to search for images that pertain to a particular phrase. You can also access an

Advanced Search page to search for images of a specific file type, a specific size, and so on.

Be aware that images returned by Google's Image Search function may be copyrighted. If you want to use an image located using Google's Image Search, you should contact the owner of the site on which the image resides for permission.

① Type **www.google.com** in your browser's address bar and press Enter.

② Click Images.

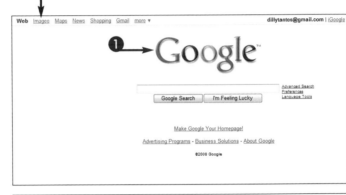

The Google Image Search page opens.

③ Type your search word or phrase.

④ Click Search Images.

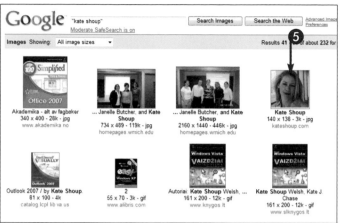

Google displays the results of your search, with thumbnail-sized images that match your search criteria.

⑤ Click a thumbnail image.

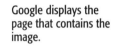

Google displays the page that contains the image.

Caution!

By default, Google's Image Search feature uses a moderate amount of filtering to omit mature content from your search results. To change the filter level, click the Advanced Image Search link to the right of the Search box and select No Filtering or Use Strict Filtering next to Safe Search. Be aware that even when using the strictest filter, some mature content may appear in your results.

You can use Google Book Search to search books for a keyword or phrase, just as you search for Web pages. Google Book Search scans through the thousands of books that libraries and publishers have made available to it to locate matches.

Depending on the level of permission granted, you may be able to see only basic information about a matching book, such as its author, publisher, and so on. Alternatively, you might see a few sentences or pages for your perusal. If the book's copyright has expired, you may be able to read the book in its entirety. Links may also be available to you to enable you to purchase the book or to locate it at your local library.

❶ Type **www.google.com** in your browser's address bar and press Enter.

❷ Click More.

❸ Click Books.

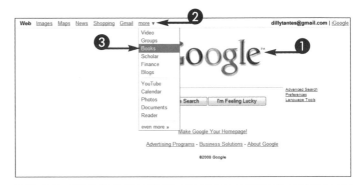

The Google Book Search page opens.

❹ Type your search word or phrase.

❺ Click Search Books.

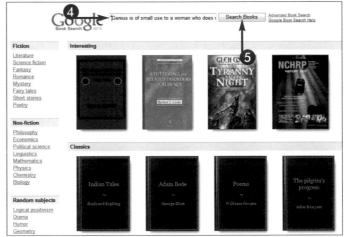

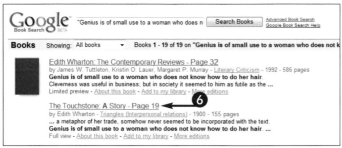

Google displays the results of your search, listing books that contain the word or phrase you typed.

⑥ Click an entry in the list.

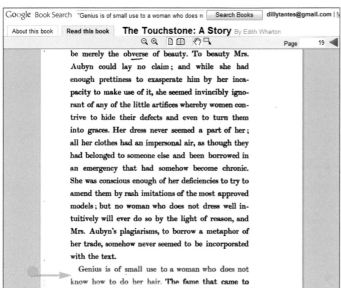

● Google displays information about the book that contains the word or phrase, and perhaps even the page itself.

More Options!

Google Book Search's My Library feature enables you to assemble a personal library, share it with friends, and label, review, and rate books in your library. To create your own library, you must have a Google account; you then simply click the Add to My Library link next to a book you want to add. For more information about My Library and creating a Google account, see Google's Help Center.

Stay Current with Google News

One main reason people use the Internet is to access news, often from multiple sources. To expedite this, Google gathers news from thousands of sources, displaying it on a single site, which you can access for free.

Google News divides news into categories, which include World, U.S., Business, Science & Technology, Sports, Entertainment, and Health,

plus Top Stories and Most Popular. You can view news by category, or search for stories by entering a keyword or phrase.

You can set up Google News to e-mail you news notifications using the parameters you specify. You might use this to follow a particular story or even receive the latest sports scores.

BROWSE NEWS BY CATEGORY

① Type **http://news. google.com** in your browser's address bar and press Enter.

② Click a news category.

A list of stories in the selected category appears.

③ Click a story link.

The site for the news source running the story opens, displaying the story text.

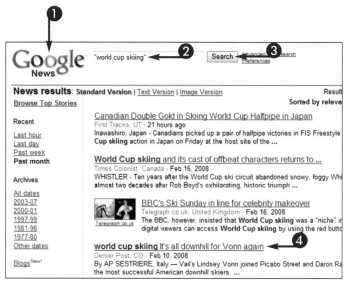

SEARCH FOR NEWS BY KEYWORD

① Type **http://news. google.com** in your browser's address bar and press Enter.

② Type a keyword or phrase.

③ Click Search.

Google News displays a list of stories that contain the keyword or phrase you typed.

④ Click a story link.

The site for the news source running the story opens, displaying the story text.

More Options!

To set up Google News to alert you via e-mail of news developments, click the News Alerts link on the Google News page, type a keyword or phrase for the topic you want to monitor, indicate what types of sites you want checked for your topic, indicate how often the sites should be checked, enter your e-mail address, and click Create Alert.

Google Maps enables you to orient yourself by viewing a map of a location you specify.

You can search for a location by entering an address, intersection, general area, the name of a landmark, the name of a person (assuming his or her contact information is listed in a public directory), the name of a business, a zip code, and so on.

In addition to viewing a map of the location you enter, you can also view a satellite image of the area, and you can zoom in and out to view a more or less detailed map or satellite image.

---

① Type **www.google.com** in your browser's address bar and press Enter.

② Click Maps.

The Google Maps page opens.

③ Type the name of a business, an address, or some other type of location information.

④ Click Search Maps.

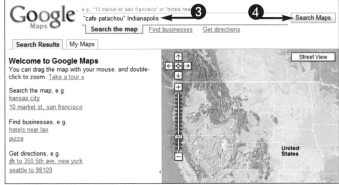

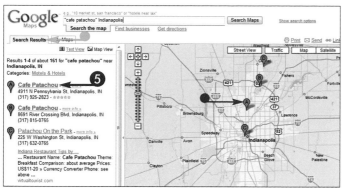

● Google displays the results of your search, listing locations that pertain to the search parameters you typed.

● A flag for each item in the list appears on the map.

⑤ Click a location.

● Google Maps displays more information about the location in a special box.

⑥ Click here as many times as necessary to zoom in.

⑦ Click Satellite to see a satellite image of the location.

More Options!

You can use Google Maps to save any maps you view. To do so, click Save to My Maps in the special box that contains information about the displayed location. Then choose My Saved Places and click Save. To access your saved maps, click the My Maps tab on the left side of the screen and click the map that you want to view in the list.

For many people, keeping track of their schedules, not to mention the schedules of their co-workers or loved ones, can be difficult. To ease your burden, Google offers an online calendar tool that you can use to set up a calendar that multiple people, such as the members of your family, can access and edit.

depending on the permissions you set, each user can view, add, and change events as needed.

To create and share a Google calendar, both you and anyone with whom you want to share the calendar must have a Google account; for information about creating a Google account, see Google's Help Center.

---

① Type **www.google. com/calendar** in your browser's address bar and press Enter.

② Click Add.

③ Click Create a New Calendar.

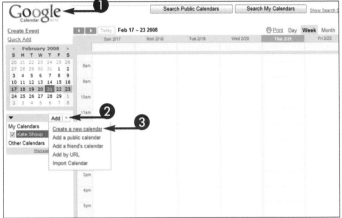

The Create New Calendar screen opens.

④ Name your calendar.

⑤ Type a description for your calendar.

⑥ Enter your geographical location.

⑦ Select the appropriate time zone for your calendar.

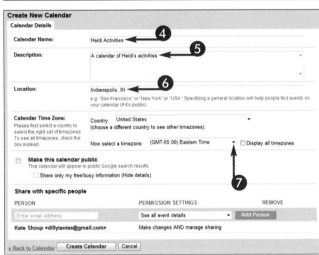

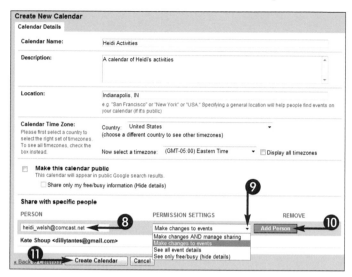

⑧ Type the e-mail address of the person with whom you want to share your calendar.

⑨ Specify the permission level you want to grant this user.

⑩ Click Add Person.

⑪ Click Create Calendar.

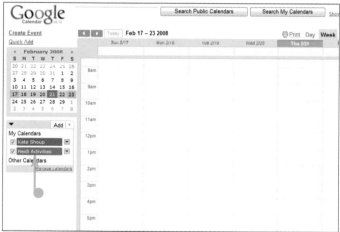

● The new calendar is added.

More Options!

A quick way to add an event to your calendar is to locate the desired day and click the time. In the box that appears, type a description, select the calendar to which the event should be added, and click Create Event. To adjust the duration of the event, position your mouse pointer over the bottom or top edge of the event calendar entry, click, and drag up or down.

Chapter 4

Entering the Blogosphere

Short for *Web log*, a *blog* is a type of Web site that enables an individual or group to share feelings, insights, and opinions. Some blogs are simply the online journal of an individual, detailing the minutiae of his or her life. Other blogs focus on a particular topic, such as politics, food, or fashion.

The Web plays host to literally millions of blogs. As great as it is to have access to such a breadth of content, however, actually finding the blog you seek can be tricky. In this chapter, you will learn how to locate and subscribe to blogs written by others.

You will also discover how easy it is to create and maintain your own blog. For example, you might do so to keep in touch with friends and family, or to further your career. Unlike a regular Web site, which requires you to learn how to use HTML or a Web editor such as FrontPage, creating and maintaining a blog involves learning just a few simple operations.

Quick Tips

The Internet boasts literally millions of blogs, covering topics that range from the minutiae of a person's daily life to such global issues as climate change. With so many blogs out there, how do you locate the one you seek?

One way is to simply search for a keyword or phrase using Google, but any blogs returned in your search results will be intermingled with — and possibly buried under — standard sites. A better approach is to use one of several blog directories to locate the blog you want. Using a blog directory (here, Blogged.com), you can browse through various categories of blogs to find one that piques your interest, or search for a specific blog using a keyword or phrase (as outlined here).

① Type **www.blogged.com** in your Web browser's address bar and press Enter.

② Type a keyword or phrase that relates to the blog you seek.

③ Click Search.

● Blogged.com displays a list of blogs that match your search criteria.

④ Click a blog in the list to view more information about it.

Blogged.com displays more information about the blog.

● Recent posts provide a sample of the blog's content.

❺ To view the blog, click its link.

The blog opens.

More Options!

If you encounter a blog you particularly like — or hate — you can add a review of that blog to Blogged.com. To do so, click the Review This Blog button in the blog's info screen on Blogged.com, type your review, click on the rating scale, and click Submit Your Review. (Note that in order to review a blog, you must sign up with Blogged.com; membership is free.)

Subscribe to a Blog

If you happen upon a blog that you particularly enjoy, you can use Internet Explorer 7 to subscribe to it — usually free of charge. When you subscribe to a blog, which is a type of *RSS feed* (*RSS*, short for Really Simple Syndication, simply refers to the technology used to create and distribute the feed) each new blog post is downloaded automatically to your Web browser.

To view a blog to which you subscribe, you need not direct your browser to the blog. Instead, you can access the subscribed blog from within Internet Explorer's Favorites Center. When you do, a special page with blog posts from the subscribed blog appears.

SUBSCRIBE TO A FEED

① With the blog to which you want to subscribe open in Internet Explorer 7, click the RSS Feed button.

Note: *If the RSS Feed button (🔲) is not visible, click the toolbar options button ( ) in the upper-right corner of your Internet Explorer 7 window to reveal it.*

② Click Subscribe to this Feed.

● An Internet Explorer dialog box opens, informing you that the feed, or blog, will be saved in the Feeds folder.

③ Click Subscribe.

Internet Explorer 7 subscribes you to the feed.

① Click the Favorites Center button to open the Favorites Center.

② Click Feeds.

③ Click the subscribed blog you want to view.

A special page with posts from the subscribed blog appears.

dillytante
Today, February 21, 2008; 45 minutes ago

Lunartic
Yesterday, February 20, 2008, 10:45:58 PM | dillytante →

But maybe the--or a--solution is to be open to wonder, and hope that the moments that transcend this sadness make up for the ones that don't? Like tonight: I stood out in the bracing cold and watched the lunar eclipse, watched the shadow of the Earth darken the moon, and it was...*worth it.*

Basal State
Yesterday, February 20, 2008, 10:15:56 PM | dillytante →

Today I sat with my friend--the one who recently miscarried--and I figured that maybe to pass the time we could watch a movie, only it had to be a) one already in my collection, because I was due at her house before the movie store opened and b) one that had absolutely no babies in it, not even a mention of one, not even one in the form of an extra on the set. So I chose "Love Actually." And I've watched it before, obviously, seeing as how I own it, but I had forgotten, I guess, that it is, uh, about *love*, which, as we know, is apparently *not* my department. And by the time it was over I basically wanted to fire up my car in the garage and nap to death.

I'm working really *really* hard to just sit with all this, to try not to run from all this sadness I feel, to convince myself that I have no more of an idea what the future holds than a goldfish, but I don't seem to be able to control my thinking about any of this. And so I feel hopeless and afraid and terribly lonely. But then, I can also see that a lot of those feelings are a direct result of my own behavior. Case in point: I have left my profile up on match.com, and I have received the occasional email from various strangers who think I seem just swell, but for the most part I cannot bring myself to respond--although I did correspond briefly with two different people, only to let my end of the dialog trail off. I don't know if I'm just being stubborn or defeatist or what, but clearly I'm not behaving in a way that is conducive to meeting someone and moving on, conducive to forgetting about S.

More Options!

Microsoft Outlook 2007 automatically retrieves posts to blogs to which you have subscribed using Internet Explorer 7. To access them, click the RSS Feeds mail folder, click the folder for the blog, and click a post in the message list to view its contents. To view the post in your Web browser, click the View Article link at the bottom of the post.

Start Your Own Blog

Suppose you want to establish a Web presence, but the thought of developing the necessary skills to create and manage a Web site — that is, learning HTML or mastering a Web site creation program such as FrontPage — seems daunting. If so, a blog may be just the thing for you.

Several Web sites on the Internet are dedicated to hosting blogs. These sites feature simple tools for creating and maintaining a blog. Perhaps the most popular blog hosting site is Blogger, covered here. To create a blog on Blogger, you must first create an account. If you already have a Google account, you can use it on Blogger; if not, Blogger gives you the chance to create one during the blog setup process, as outlined here.

① Type **www.blogger.com** in your Web browser's address bar and press Enter.

② Click Create Your Blog Now.

③ Type and retype your e-mail address.

④ Type and retype the password you want to use to access your blog account.

● Blogger assesses the strength of your password.

⑤ Type the name you want to use to sign blog posts.

⑥ Type the characters you see in the picture.

⑦ Select the I Accept the Terms of Service check box.

⑧ Click Continue.

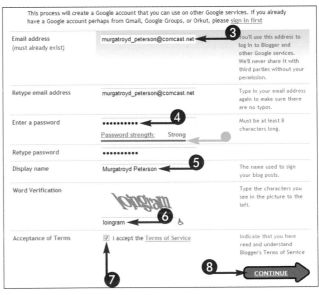

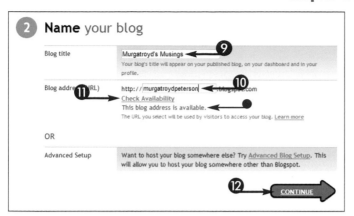

2 Name your blog

Blog title · Murgatroyd's Musings — ⑨

Your blog's title will appear on your published blog, on your dashboard and in your profile.

Blog addre⑪RL) · http://murgatroydpeterson — blogspot.com ⑩
Check Availability
This blog address is available. ←
The URL you select will be used by visitors to access your blog. Learn more

OR

Advanced Setup · Want to host your blog somewhere else? Try Advanced Blog Setup. This will allow you to host your blog somewhere other than Blogspot.

⑫ CONTINUE →

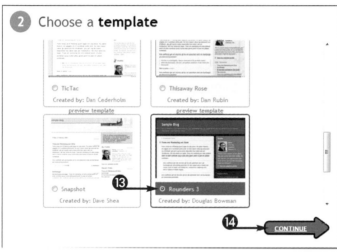

2 Choose a template

○ TicTac — Created by: Dan Cederholm — preview template
○ Thisaway Rose — Created by: Dan Rubin — preview template
○ Snapshot — Created by: Dave Shea — ⑬
○ Rounders 3 — Created by: Douglas Bowman

⑭ CONTINUE →

⑨ Type the title you want for your blog.

⑩ Type the Web address you want for your blog.

⑪ To ensure that the Web address you typed is available, click Check Availability.

● Blogger confirms that this address is available.

⑫ Click Continue.

Blogger offers several predesigned blog templates.

⑬ Click the template you want to use for your blog.

⑭ Click Continue.

Blogger creates your blog and sends an e-mail to the e-mail account you entered during the blog creation process, asking you to activate your account and verify your e-mail address by clicking a link in the message.

 TIP

Caution!

Unless you take steps to make your blog private (see the tip in the task "Create a New Post" for details), your posts will be available for public view. That means if you write something unflattering about a person, there is a chance of that person seeing what you have written if he or she happens upon your blog. Be discreet!

Populate Your Profile

One of the first things you should do after creating a blog is populate your profile. That way, people visiting your blog can learn a little bit about you. Your profile can be as spare or as detailed as you choose; this task points out some of the more common portrait details.

Before you can populate your profile, you must log in to your blog to access the Blogger

Dashboard, which provides access to various blogging tools. One way to log in is by entering your e-mail address and password in the fields provided on Blogger's main page. (Access Blogger's main page by typing **www.blogger.com** in your browser's address bar or typing your blog's Web address and clicking the Sign In link.)

---

① In the Blogger Dashboard, click Edit Profile.

The Edit User Profile page opens.

② Select this check box to display your profile on your blog.

③ Select this check box to reveal your name.

④ Select this check box to reveal your e-mail address.

⑤ To use a different e-mail address from the one you use to sign in, type it here.

⑥ If you want to reveal your name to blog visitors, type it here.

● You can add a photo to your profile; to locate and select it, click Browse.

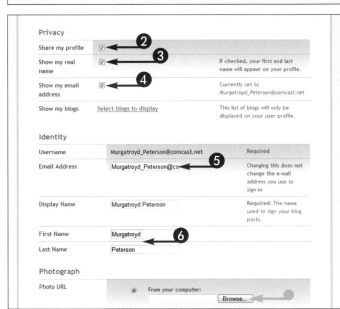

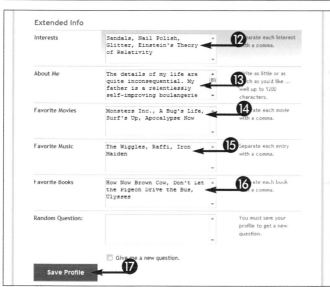

⑦ Choose Female or Male.

⑧ Type your date of birth.

⑨ Select this check box if you want your profile to include your astrological sign.

⑩ Type your geographical location.

⑪ Specify your line of work.

⑫ Cite your interests.

⑬ Provide a bio containing as many as 1,200 characters.

⑭ List your favorite movies.

⑮ Type your favorite music.

⑯ Type your favorite books.

Note: *When typing your interests and your favorite movies, music, and books, separate each entry with a comma.*

⑰ Click Save Profile.

TIP

More Options!

When people visit your blog, certain parts of your profile appear on screen. In addition to displaying this profile text, you can also display a description of your blog. To do so, click the Settings link in the Blogger Dashboard and, in the Basic screen, type the desired text in the Description field and click Save Settings at the bottom of the screen.

During the blog setup process, you are asked to select a template, which serves to define the look and feel of your blog. For example, the blog shown in this task uses the Rounders 3 template.

If the template you choose does not quite suit you, you can easily choose a different one. In addition, you can modify your chosen template by changing the colors and fonts used and by moving screen elements around.

As you work, you can preview changes to your template before saving them. This enables you to try out lots of different settings to determine which ones offer the best result.

---

① In the Blogger Dashboard, click Layout.

Note: To access the Blogger Dashboard, you must log in to your blog by entering your e-mail address and password in the fields provided on Blogger's main page.

The Add and Arrange Page Elements page opens.

② Click a page element and drag it to a new location.

● Click Add a Page Element to add one of several page elements.

● Click Edit to edit a page element.

● Click Preview to preview the change.

● Click Clear Edits to undo the change.

③ Click Save.

Blogger saves your changes.

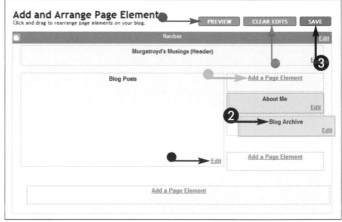

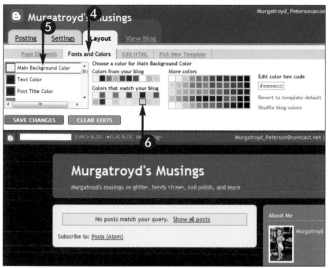

④ Click Fonts and Colors.

⑤ Click the template element whose color you want to change.

⑥ Click a new color for the template element.

● The new color is applied to the selected template element.

⑦ Click the template element whose font you want to change.

⑧ Click a different font.

⑨ Click Smaller or Larger to change the font's size.

● Your font changes are applied.

⑩ Click Save Changes.

   Blogger saves your changes.

More Options!
In addition to moving screen elements, you can also add new ones, including the following: a photo slideshow, an interactive poll feature, a list (for example, of your favorite foods), text, video clips, and more. To do so, click any of the Add a Page Element links in the Add and Arrange Page Elements screen, select the type of element you want to add, and follow the on-screen instructions.

Unlike most Web sites, which are static entities, blogs are meant to be updated; readers visit often with the expectation of finding fresh material. Many bloggers add new posts multiple times each day. Fortunately, Blogger makes it easy to create new posts, and even offers tools such as spell-check to help you put your best foot forward.

Note that you can format the text in your post in any number of ways. For example, you can change the font, font size, and font color; apply bold and italics; left-align, center-align, right-align, and justify text; format text as a bulleted or numbered list; and convert text to a block quote. The next task discusses how to use these tools.

① In the Blogger Dashboard, click New Post.

Note: *To access the Blogger Dashboard, you must log in to your blog by entering your e-mail address and password in the fields provided on Blogger's main page.*

② Type a title for your post.

③ Type the body of the post.

● Click here to run a spell check.

④ Click Publish Post.

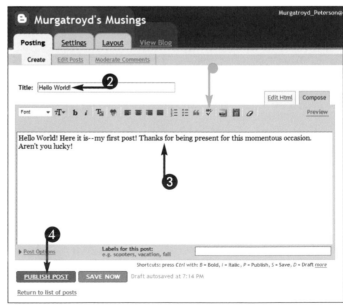

Blogger publishes the post.

⑤ To view the post, click View Blog.

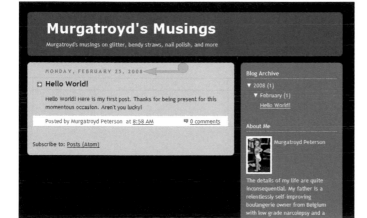

● The post appears on your blog.

More Options!

By default, your blog posts will be available for public view. To make your blog private, you can restrict it to readers you choose. To do so, click Settings in the Dashboard, click Permissions, and click Only People I Choose under Blog Readers. Finally, type the e-mail addresses of people you want to invite to your blog, and click Invite.

Suppose, after reading a post on your blog, you want to make some changes to it — for example, clarify a point, or format the text in the post differently. Blogger makes it easy to do so.

In addition to editing posts that have published, you can also edit posts that you have saved as drafts. You might save a post as a draft if, for example, you do not have time to finish writing during your current session. To save a post as a draft, simply click Save Now in the screen where you compose your posts. Posts that have been saved as drafts are clearly marked in the Edit Posts screen shown in this task.

① In the Blogger Dashboard, click Posts.

Note: *To access the Blogger Dashboard, you must log in to your blog by entering your e-mail address and password in the fields provided on Blogger's main page.*

The Edit Posts screen appears.

● Drafts are so marked here.

② Locate the post you want to change and click Edit.

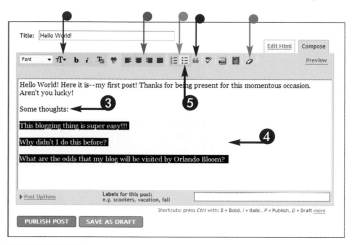

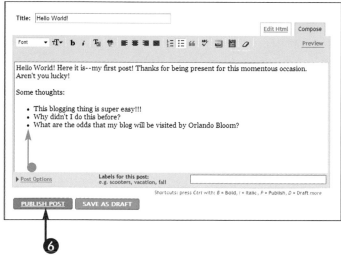

❸ Edit your text.

❹ To format text, select the text you want to change.

● Click here to change the font or size, apply bold or italics, or alter the font color.

● Click here to change the text's alignment.

● Click here to format the text as a numbered or bulleted list.

● Click here to format the text as a block quote.

● Click here to undo any formatting.

❺ Click the bulleted list button.

● The text is formatted as a bulleted list.

❻ Click Publish Post.

Blogger updates the post with your changes.

Remove It!

If you no longer want a post to appear on your blog, you can delete it. To delete a post, click Posts in the Blogger Dashboard, locate the post you want to delete in the Edit Posts screen, and click the Delete link on the right side of the post's entry. When prompted, click Delete to confirm the operation; the post disappears from your blog.

Add a Photo to a Post

One sure-fire way to boost interest in your blog is to feature photographs — especially if you intend for family and friends to view your blog. Fortunately, Blogger makes adding snapshots a snap.

When you add a photo, you have the option of specifying where on the page the photo should appear, and how large it should be. You can also indicate whether the settings you choose should be applied by default anytime you add a photo in the future. Photos can be ones that live on the Internet or that are stored on your computer's hard drive (as outlined here).

---

1 With the post to which you want to add a photo open in the Create screen or the Edit Post screen, click the Add Image button.

2 Type the photo's file path and name.

● If you do not know the file path and name, click Browse, navigate to the folder containing the photo, and click it.

3 Specify where on the page the photo should appear.

4 Choose a photo size.

● Select this check box if you want to use this layout by default.

5 Select the I Accept the Terms of Service check box.

Note: *This check box appears only the first time you upload an image.*

6 Click Upload Image.

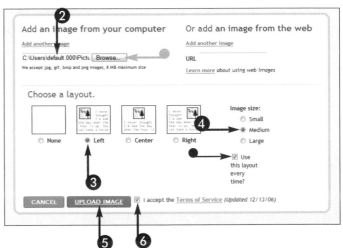

Your image has been added.

After clicking "Done" you can change your post and publish to your blog.

DONE ← ⑦

Blogger uploads the image.

⑦ Click Done.

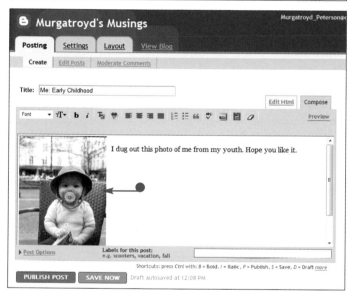

● The image is added to your post; complete the entry and publish it as normal.

Note: *You can resize the image by clicking it in this screen and dragging any of the sizing handles that appear around the image.*

Remove It!
You can remove a photo from a post. To do so, open the post in the Edit Posts screen (or, if you have yet to publish the post or save it as a draft, in the Create screen), click the image to select it, and then press the Delete key on your keyboard.

Add a Video to a Post

Videos can go a long way toward enlivening your blog. People visiting your site can view the posted video with the click of a mouse.

With Blogger, uploading a video stored on your hard drive is a simple operation. Supported video file types include AVI, MPEG, QuickTime, Real, and Windows Media.

Note that uploading a video to a post can be time consuming because video files tend to be quite large (although Blogger does impose a maximum size of 100MB). Just how long the upload operation takes depends on two factors: the size of your video and the speed of your Internet connection. As the upload occurs, a placeholder will appear in your post.

① With the post to which you want to add a video open in the Create screen or the Edit Post screen, click the Add Video button.

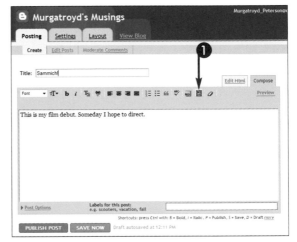

The Add a Video to Your Blog dialog box appears.

② Click Browse.

The Choose File dialog box appears.

③ Locate and click the video you want to add.

④ Click Open.

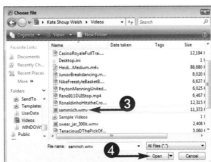

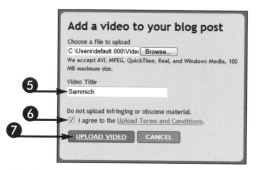

Add a video to your blog post

Choose a file to upload

C:\Users\default.000\Vide| [Browse...]

We accept AVI, MPEG, QuickTime, Real, and Windows Media, 100 MB maximum size.

Video Title

Sammich

Do not upload infringing or obscene material.

☑ I agree to the Upload Terms and Conditions.

[UPLOAD VIDEO]   [CANCEL]

⑤ Type a title for the video.

⑥ Select the I Agree to the Upload Terms and Conditions check box.

Note: *This check box appears only the first time you upload a video.*

⑦ Click Upload Video.

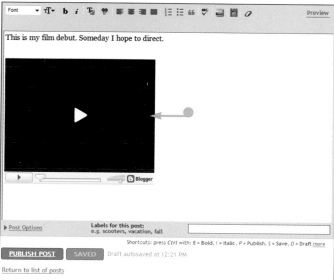

This is my film debut. Someday I hope to direct.

● The video is added to your post; complete the entry and publish it as normal.

Note: *To view the video, anyone visiting your page simply needs to click the Play button that appears alongside the video.*

More Options!

To post a video from YouTube on your blog, locate the video on YouTube and click the Share button on the video's page on YouTube. If this is your first attempt at sharing a YouTube video, scroll down on the page, click Set Up Your Blog for Video Posting, choose Add a Blog/Site, select Blogger as your blog service, enter your Google account login information, and select your blog.

Insert a Hyperlink in a Post

As you blog, you may find yourself referring to other sites on the Internet — for example, news sites, video-hosting pages, or other blogs. You can add a hyperlink to one of these Web sources to your own blog; people reading your blog can then simply click the link to view the item you are discussing.

In many cases, you can simply copy a site's URL and paste it as a link into one of your posts. Another option, outlined here, is to click the Link button in either the Create screen or the Edit Post screen in Blogger. Yet another option is to use the Send To Blogger option on the Google Toolbar, outlined in the tip at the end of this task.

---

① With the post to which you want to add a link open in the Create screen or the Edit Post screen, click the Link button.

● The Hyperlink dialog box opens.

② Click the Type ▾ and select the type of page to which you want to link.

Note: In most cases, the default, http:, is correct.

③ Type the site's Web address.

④ Click OK.

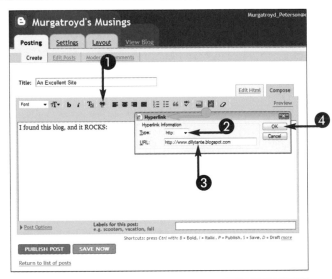

● The link appears in your post.

⑤ Click Publish Post.

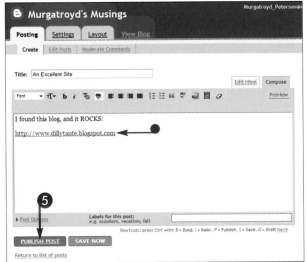

6 To view the link on your blog, click View Blog.

● The link is shown in the blog post.

Try This!

If you have installed the Google Toolbar in your browser (refer to "Install and Use the Google Toolbar" in Chapter 3), you can add a link to your blog by opening the page to which you want to link, clicking the Send To button, and choosing Blogger from the list that appears. A new post is created that contains the link to the page.

Allow Additional Blog Contributors

Suppose you want to allow others to contribute to your blog, making it a group effort. For example, you might open your blog for contributions by your family members. Fortunately, Blogger makes it easy to allow others to contribute posts to your blog — as many as 100 people can participate.

When you invite someone to contribute to your blog, Blogger sends that person an e-mail message that contains a link; he or she must click the link to accept your invitation. (Note that anyone who contributes to your blog must possess a Google account; invitees are given the chance to create one when they accept your invitation.)

① In the Blogger Dashboard, click Settings.

Note: To access the Blogger Dashboard, you must log in to your blog by entering your e-mail address and password in the fields provided on Blogger's main page.

② Click Permissions.
③ Click Add Authors.

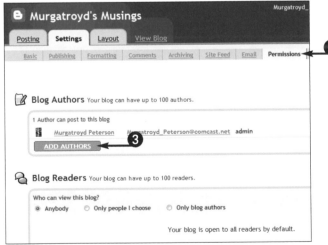

④ Type the potential contributor's e-mail address.

⑤ Click Invite.

Blogger sends the potential contributor an e-mail invitation.

● When the contributor accepts the e-mail invitation, he or she is listed in the Blog Authors area.

More Options!

Additional contributors are given "Author" privileges, meaning they can add posts and edit the ones they have authored. You can upgrade their privileges to "Admin," enabling them to perform such administrative tasks as managing comments, adding and deleting authors, and so on. To do so, click Grant Admin Privileges next to the contributor's name in the Blog Authors area.

Attract Readers to Your Blog

If you want to attract readers to your blog, there are a few steps you can take. One is to enter your blog in various blog directories (covered in the next task). Another perhaps more effective approach is to generate word of mouth.

Of course, you might start by telling your friends, family, and colleagues about your blog and asking them to pass it on. Also, you could

add your blog's Web address to your business cards. A third option is to add a link to your blog to all of your e-mail messages (covered here using Microsoft Outlook 2007). This not only spreads the word about your blog to everyone with whom you communicate via e-mail, but also gives them direct access to your writing.

---

① In Microsoft Outlook 2007, click Tools.

② Click Options.

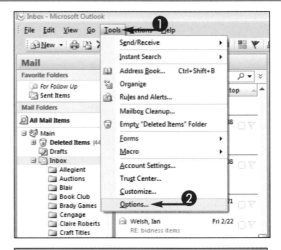

The Options dialog box opens.

③ Click Mail Format.

④ Click Signatures.

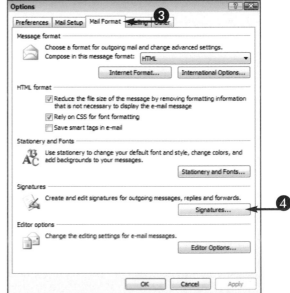

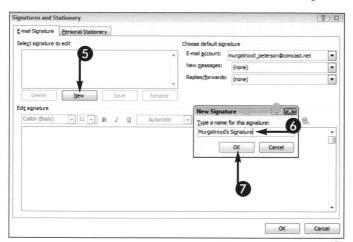

The Signatures and Stationery dialog box opens, displaying the E-mail Signature tab.

5 Click New.

● The New Signature dialog box opens.

6 Type a name for the signature you want to create.

7 Click OK.

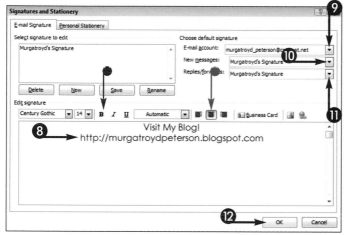

8 Type your signature's text.

● Use these tools to adjust the font.

● Click any of these buttons to align the text.

9 Click the E-mail Account ▾ and specify the e-mail account to which the signature should apply.

10 Click the New Messages ▾ and choose the signature's name.

11 Click the Replies/Forwards ▾ and choose the signature's name.

12 Click OK.

13 Click OK to close the Options dialog box.

Try This!

Another way to generate interest in your blog is to trade links with other bloggers — that is, ask them to place a link to your blog on their blog if you do the same for them. To add a link to your blog's sidebar (as opposed to simply inserting one in a post), click Add a Page Element in the Page Elements screen, choose Link List, and follow the on-screen instructions.

Although the occasional visitor may find your blog by conducting a search on, say, Google for a word or phrase that appears in your blog, the fact is that the Internet plays host to millions of active blogs — meaning that the odds of a potential reader happening onto yours are slim.

To better the chances that your blog will become more broadly read, you should list it with various blog directories, like the one discussed in the task "Search for Blogs" earlier in this chapter.

This task demonstrates how to add your blog to Blogged, although there are several other blog directories online to which you should add your blog. (Conduct a search for "blog directory" on Google to locate more.)

---

① Type **www.blogged.com** in your Web browser's address bar and press Enter.

② Click Submit a Blog.

The Blog Information screen appears.

③ Type your blog's title.

④ Type your blog's Web address.

⑤ Click the Primary Category ▼ and select the category that best describes your blog's content.

⑥ Click the Secondary Category ▼ and select the second-most-descriptive category.

7 Type descriptive tags here.

Note: *If someone searches for a blog on Blogged.com using one or more words you entered as a tag, your blog will be returned as a match.*

8 Type a description for your blog.

9 Optionally, type your e-mail address.

10 Click Submit Blog.

Blogged.com displays a screen notifying you that your blog has been submitted, and that it will be reviewed and posted as quickly as possible.

Did You Know?

As more people find your blog, you may find it useful to include a hit counter on it, as well as to gather information about your visitors such as their location, which pages they viewed, and so on. One useful tool that enables you to do this and more is Stat Counter; for more information, visit the Stat Counter Web site at www.statcounter.com.

Moderate Blog Comments

By default, comments are enabled on Blogger; anyone with a Google account can leave comments about posts on your blog. For example, readers might submit comments to provide feedback on your writing or to offer advice. Typically, comments appear just below the post to which they relate.

If you want, you can expand permissions to allow anyone — not just those with Google accounts — to leave comments. You can also configure your blog to not publish comments that are submitted until you approve them. Moderating comments in this way enables you to ensure that no overly inflammatory comments are revealed to your readers, as well as prevent spam in the form of comments from appearing on your blog.

ENABLE COMMENT MODERATION

① In the Blogger Dashboard, click Settings.

The Settings page opens.

② Click Comments.

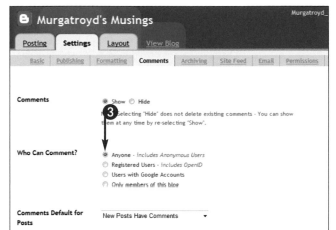

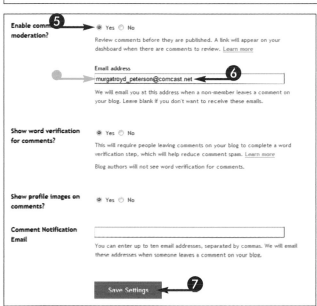

The Comments screen appears.

③ To change who is permitted to comment, select a different option here.

④ Scroll down the page.

⑤ Click Yes next to Enable Comment Moderation.

● An Email Address field appears.

⑥ If you want new comments to be e-mailed to you, type your e-mail address here.

⑦ Click Save Settings.

Blogger enables comment moderation.

Did You Know?

To leave a comment on a blog, simply click the Comments link below the post on which you want to comment. In the screen that appears, type your comment, enter your Google user name and password (if required) or select a different ID form (if available), and click Publish Your Comment.

When comment moderation is enabled, you are given the opportunity to publish or reject any comments that are submitted. Depending on the settings you choose, the comment may be e-mailed to you, in which case you can publish or reject the comment by clicking the appropriate link in the e-mail message; otherwise, you can publish or reject comments from the Blogger Dashboard.

Similar to comments are *backlinks*. When you set up the feature that enables backlinks, you can easily determine when someone has linked to a post on your blog from his or her own page. Backlinks are discussed further in the tip at the end of this task.

MODERATE COMMENTS

① In the Blogger Dashboard, click *x* Comments.

The Moderate Comments screen appears.

② Select the check box next to the comment you want to moderate.

● Click Publish to publish the comment.

● Click Reject to reject the comment.

Blogger confirms that the publish or reject operation is complete.

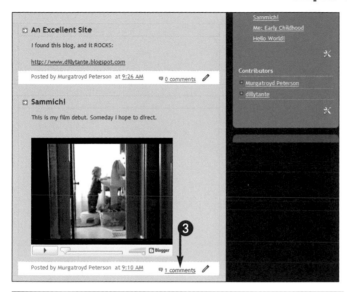

❸ To view a published comment, click *x* Comments beneath the post to which the comment refers.

● The comment appears.

● You can reply to the comment; type your reply here and click Publish Your Comment at the bottom of the screen.

More Options!

If someone adds a link to a post on your blog to his or her own site, you can view that link on that person's site by clicking Links to This Post under the post on your blog and clicking the link to the site that appears. (To disable this feature, called Backlinks, click Settings in the Dashboard, click Comments, and click Hide next to the Backlinks entry.)

5

Managing and Sharing Photos Online

If you have a digital camera, you can use Flickr to organize and share your photos online, as well as order prints of your favorites — all free of charge (although you can upgrade to Flickr's enhanced paid site for added services).

Using Flickr's free site, you can upload as many as 100 megabytes of photos per month. Although there is no limit to the number of photos you can store on Flickr using a free account, only the 200 most recently uploaded images will be displayed. (The paid site offers unlimited image display.)

Once your images have been uploaded, you can add titles, descriptions, and tags to them; organize them into sets and collections; apply content filters; and edit them using Flickr's Web-based editing tool, called Picnik.

Flickr is more than a site that enables you to manage your own photos, however. It also enables you to connect with others. For example, you can create a Flickr profile to share your interests with other Flickr users. You can also add contacts to a special Flickr address book, and send invitations to your contacts to view your images. You can even enable others to comment on your photos.

Quick Tips

Create a Flickr Account

In order to use Flickr, you must first create a Yahoo! account. Fortunately, doing so is easy. You enter your name and a few other informational tidbits such as your gender, date of birth, country of residence, and postal code; choose a user name (called a Yahoo! ID), password, and security question and answer (to be used in the event you forget your password); enter a backup e-mail address; type the special code that appears; and agree to Flickr's terms of service.

If you already have a Yahoo! account, you can simply sign in to Flickr using your account user name and password. You need not create a separate Flickr account.

---

① Type **www.flickr.com** in your Web browser's address bar.

② Click Create Your Account.

③ Click Sign Up.

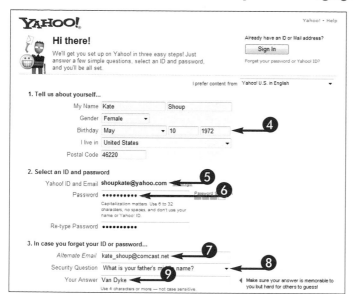

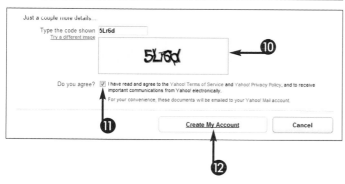

④ Type your first and last name, your gender, your birth date, and your geographical location.

⑤ Select a Yahoo! ID.

⑥ Type and retype the password you want to use.

⑦ Enter an alternate e-mail address.

⑧ Choose a security question.

⑨ Type the answer to the selected security question.

⑩ Type the code shown.

⑪ Select the Do You Agree check box.

⑫ Click Create My Account.

Your Yahoo! account is created.

Important!

After you create your account, Yahoo! sends you a confirmation e-mail message. When you receive the message, open it, and click the link contained in the message to activate the account. Flickr launches a special confirmation Web page; choose a screen name for the account on the page (this does not have to be the same as your Yahoo! ID) and click Create a New Account.

Upload Digital Images to Flickr

To share and organize your photos on Flickr, you must first upload them to the site. One way is to use Flickr's downloadable upload software tools; another is to use the site's Web-based upload tool (covered here). In addition, you can e-mail photos to your Flickr account from your computer or your phone. (When you e-mail images, the message's subject line becomes the photo's title and the body text becomes the description. Titles and descriptions are discussed later.)

Files you upload to Flickr can be as large as 5MB (for the free Flickr site) or 10MB (for the paid version). Supported photo file types include JPEG, GIF, PNG, and TIFF (although TIFF files are converted to and stored as JPEGs).

---

1 While signed in to Flickr, click Upload Photos on the main page.

Note: *To sign in to Flickr, click the Sign In link in the upper right corner of the main Flickr page, type your Yahoo! ID (if it is not already displayed), type your password, and click Sign In.*

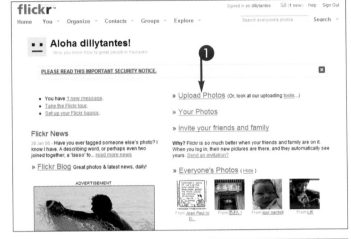

2 Click Choose Photos.

● The Select Files to Upload by www.flickr.com dialog box opens.

3 Locate and select the pictures you want to upload.

4 Click Open.

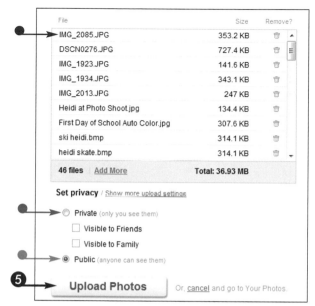

- The photos you selected for upload appear in a list.

- Select Private and then select Visible to Friends and/or Visible to Family to limit viewing of your pictures to friends and family only.

- Select Public (the default setting) to make your pictures visible to everyone.

⑤ Click Upload Photos.

   Flickr uploads your photos.

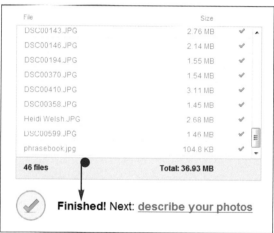

- Flickr notifies you when the upload process is complete.

Note: *To immediately add tags, titles, and descriptions to your photos, click Describe Your Photos. Alternatively, you can add them at a later time, as outlined in the task "Add Titles, Descriptions, and Tags" later in this chapter.*

More Options!

To upload images via e-mail from your phone or computer, you must use the unique e-mail upload address Flickr creates for you. To prompt Flickr to create it, click the You ▾ on your main Flickr page, click Your Account, click the E-mail tab, and click Create an Upload to Flickr E-mail Address.

Add Titles, Descriptions, and Tags

Your pictures tell a story — and that story can be made all the more entertaining with titles and descriptions. You can easily add titles and descriptions to the images you upload onto Flickr, either when you upload your photos or at the time of your choosing (as covered here).

You can also add tags to your photos. Tags are like keywords; you add them to a photo to make it easier to find. For example, you might

tag all photos taken during your vacation with the word "vacation." Alternatively, you might tag all photos of a specific person with that person's name.

You can expedite the creation of titles, descriptions, and tags by first gathering the photos you want to edit into batches using the Flickr Organizr.

---

① While signed in to Flickr, click Organize on the main page.

Note: *To sign in to Flickr, click the Sign In link in the upper right corner of the main Flickr page, type your Yahoo! ID (if it is not already displayed), type your password, and click Sign In.*

● The Flickr Organizr opens to the Batch Organize tab.

● Images you have uploaded to Flickr appear in the photostream.

● Click here to move forward through the photostream.

● Click here to move backward through the photostream.

② Click an image to which you want to add a title, description, or tag.

③ Drag the image to the workspace and release the mouse button.

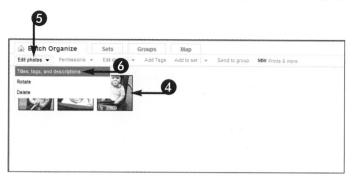

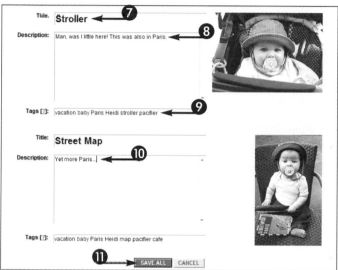

④ Drag additional images to the batch as needed.

⑤ Click Edit Photos.

⑥ Click Titles, Tags, and Descriptions.

⑦ Type a title for an image.

⑧ Type a description for the image.

⑨ Type tags for the image.

Note: *To enter a phrase as a tag, surround the words comprising the phrase with quotation marks.*

⑩ Repeat Steps 7 to 9 for the other images in the batch.

⑪ Click Save All.

Flickr saves the changes.

Note: *Click Thanks in the dialog box that appears to complete the operation.*

More Options!

You can also add *geotags* to your images; these show people where the image was taken. To add a geotag, click Organize on the main Flickr page, click the Map tab, and use the Pan/Zoom tools to locate the spot where the photo was taken. Then click the image in the photostream that you want to tag and drag it onto the map.

Organize Your Photos with Sets

Your Flickr photostream displays images you have uploaded to the site in the order in which they were added. You may find, however, that you would like to group your images together. For example, you might want to place all images from a specific event together. To do so, you can create a set to house those images. The set can be given a title and description;

you can also select a specific image as the primary photo for your set, which will be displayed alongside any links to your set that appear in Flickr.

If you have a free Flickr account, you can create as many as three sets. Upgrading to a paid account enables you to create an unlimited number of sets.

---

① While signed in to Flickr, click Organize on the main page.

Note: *To sign in to Flickr, click the Sign In link in the upper right corner of the main Flickr page, type your Yahoo! ID (if it is not already displayed), type your password, and click Sign In.*

The Flickr Organizr opens.

② Click the Sets tab.

③ Click Create New Set.

④ Click the photo in the photostream that you want to use as the set's primary image.

Note: *The primary image appears both over the square in the upper left corner and in the main workspace area.*

⑤ Drag the photo over the square in the upper left corner of the screen and release the mouse button.

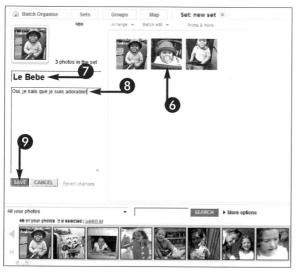

⑥ Add more images to the set by clicking them in the photostream and dragging them to the main workspace area.

⑦ Type a title for the set.

⑧ Type a description for the set.

⑨ Click Save.

Flickr saves the set.

More Options!

You can edit a set by double-clicking it in the Sets tab. The set opens in its own tab; from there, you can rearrange the photos in the set, edit tags, filters, and so on, and even order prints. To remove a photo from a set, click it in the set and drag the photo down to the photostream. Delete a set by clicking Batch Edit and clicking Delete This Set.

View Your Photos and Sets

The primary reason you use Flickr is most likely to view your photos. You can view them as you would a photo album, with several on the screen at one time, on the Your Photos page. To get a closer look at a particular image, you can simply click it on the Your Photos screen. Alternatively, you can view your images as a slideshow.

The Your Photos page also enables you to view your sets; simply click the set you want to view, and the photos in that set appear on-screen. To view an individual photo within a set, click it after opening the set.

① While signed in to Flickr, click Your Photos on the main page.

Note: *To sign in to Flickr, click the Sign In link in the upper right corner of the main Flickr page, type your Yahoo! ID (if it is not already displayed), type your password, and click Sign In.*

The Your Photos page appears.

● Photos you have uploaded appear here.

● Sets you have created appear here.

② Click View as Slideshow.

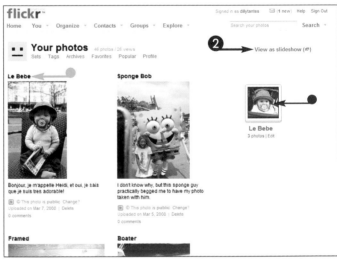

Your photos appear in a slideshow, with each one displayed for a given duration.

● Click Slow, Medium, or Fast to change how long each photo appears.

● Click the right or left arrow to move to the next or previous image manually.

❸ Click Back to Your Photos to return to the Your Photos page.

❹ Click a photo in the Your Photos screen.

● The photo appears in its own screen.

More Options!

If you want, you can change the layout of the page on which your photos are displayed. To do so, click the Your Photos link on the main Flickr screen, scroll to the bottom of the page that appears, and click the Change the Layout of This Page link. The Your Photos Page Layout page opens; select the desired layout and click Save.

Edit a Photo with Picnik

Even the best digital photographer likely needs to edit his or her photos. For example, you may find that your image lacks contrast, or the color seems slightly off, or the photo is a bit blurry. Or you might discover that your angelic subject appears with devilish red eyes in your image, requiring correction. Or maybe you just think the image would look better if it were cropped, or that it needs to be a different size.

You can make all these adjustments using Flickr's special Web-based editing software, called Picnik. Picnik also enables you to run a single auto-correct operation to rectify multiple image problems at once, as outlined here.

---

1 In the Your Photos page, click the image you want to edit.

Note: *For help viewing the Your Photos page, see the preceding task.*

2 Click Edit Photo.

Note: *If this is the first time you have used Flickr to edit a photo, you will be asked whether it is okay to open Picnik within your Flickr account. Click OK.*

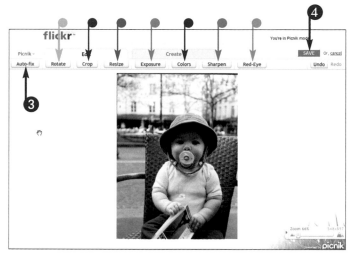

- In Picnik mode, click Rotate to rotate your photo.

- Click Crop to crop your photo.

- Click Resize to change the photo's dimensions.

- Click Exposure to change the photo's exposure levels and contrast.

- Click Colors to change the photo's color cast.

- Click Sharpen to sharpen the image.

- Click Red-Eye to fix red eye.

③ Click Auto-Fix, and Picnik corrects the image.

④ Click Save.

⑤ In the Save This Photo dialog box, click Save.

Attention!

When you edit an image using Picnik, Flickr saves it as a copy, leaving the original image intact. If you prefer the edited version, simply delete the original by clicking it in the Your Photos screen to view it in its own screen, and then clicking the Delete button. When Flickr asks you to confirm the deletion, click Yes.

If you reside in the United States and have a major credit card, you can order photo prints from Flickr. Your photos can be delivered via mail to your home, or they can be picked up from your local Target store. (Mail delivery takes longer, but tends to be slightly cheaper.)

Note that before you can print your photos, you must set your printing preferences. Flickr

prompts you to do so when you initiate the printing process for the first time; simply follow the on-screen instructions.

You can launch a print operation by opening a photo you want to print from the Your Photos screen (outlined in this task) or from the Flickr Organizr (described in the tip following this task).

---

① With the image for which you want to order a print displayed, click Prints & More.

Note: *For help displaying the photo you want to print, refer to the task "View Your Photos and Sets."*

A menu of print options appears.

② Click the ▾ next to the desired size and choose the number of prints you want.

③ Click Add to Cart.

Man, was I little here! This was also in Paris.

● To add more photos to your print order, click Continue Browsing.

④ To initiate the checkout process, click Proceed to Cart.

● Another way to initiate checkout is to click the Shopping Cart button.

- The prints you have selected appear here.

⑤ Click to select a delivery method.

⑥ Click Check Out.

Follow the on-screen instructions.

Note: *The precise steps for placing your order vary depending on what you select in Step 5, but expect to enter your address, credit card number, and so on.*

- Flickr displays an order summary.

⑦ Click Send Order.

Flickr places your order.

More Options!

Another — perhaps quicker — way to launch a print order is to use the Flickr Organizr. Click Organize on the main Flickr page and, in the Batch Organize tab that is displayed by default, drag the images you want to print onto the photostream to the main workspace. Then click the Prints & More button and follow the on-screen instructions.

Flickr is more than just a site that enables you to organize your photos; it is an online community where members can view each other's images. As such, you must ensure that potentially offensive images are not available for general viewing on Flickr.

To aid you in this, Flickr supports the use of three different safety levels: Safe, for content

that is suitable for all; Restricted, for content that kids should absolutely not see; and Moderate, for images in between. The setting you apply affects whether your image turns up in general search results performed by others.

You can establish a default safety-level setting for all images you upload, as well as change safety levels on a case-by-case basis.

---

① While signed into Flickr, click the You ▾ on the main page.

Note: *To sign in to Flickr, click the Sign In link in the upper right corner of the main Flickr page, type your Yahoo! ID (if it is not already displayed), type your password, and click Sign In.*

A menu appears.

② Click Your Account.

③ Click Privacy & Permissions.

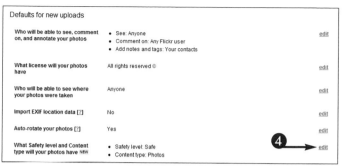

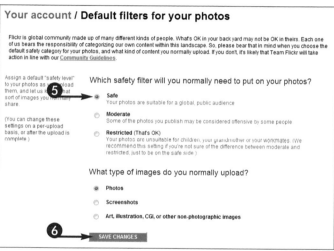

④ Next to What Safety Level and Content Type Will Your Photos Have, click Edit.

Note: *You may need to scroll down to see this option.*

⑤ Click the desired default safety level.

⑥ Click Save Changes.

Flickr saves your changes.

More Options!

To change the safety level of a particular image, click it in the Your Photos page, scroll down and click the Flag Your Photo link, select the desired safety level from among the options that appear, optionally select the Hide This Photo from Public Searches check box to prevent other users from finding your photo, and click Save.

Create Your Flickr Profile

Although you are by no means required to create a Flickr profile — indeed, all that is required of you to establish a presence on Flickr is to provide a screen name and an e-mail address — doing so better enables you to connect with other Flickr users who share your interests. If you want to take advantage

of being a part of the Flickr community, then creating a profile is a smart move.

By default, if you provide your e-mail and IM address on your profile, they are visible to your friends and family only; other information you choose to provide, such as your real name, city, and so on, are visible to everyone.

---

① While signed into Flickr, click the You ⌄ on the main page.

Note: *To sign in to Flickr, click the Sign In link in the upper right corner of the main Flickr page, type your Yahoo! ID (if it is not already displayed), type your password, and click Sign In.*

A menu appears.

② Click Your Profile.

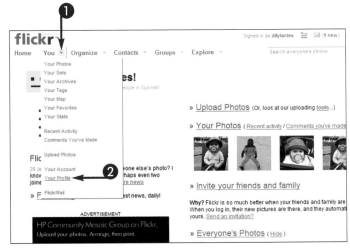

③ Click Edit Your Profile.

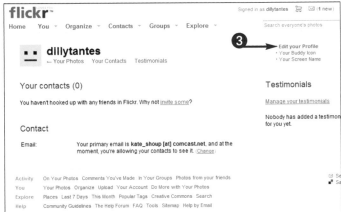

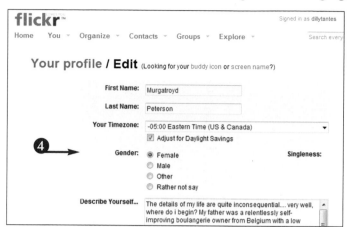

The Your Profile/Edit page appears.

④ Enter as much or as little personal information as you want.

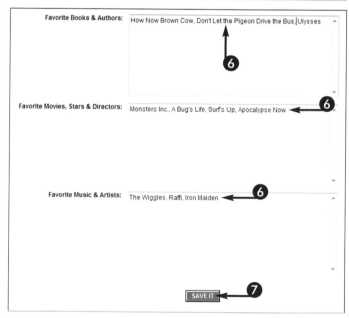

⑤ Click the scroll box and drag it downward to view the rest of the Your Profile/Edit page.

⑥ Enter any additional information.

⑦ Click Save It.

Flickr saves the changes to your profile.

More Options!

To replace the default buddy icon — the gray smiley face that appears alongside your screen name — with a photo from your Flickr photostream, click Your Buddy Icon on your profile page, click In Your Flickr Photos, click the desired image, drag the square that appears to the portion of the image you want to use (resize the square by dragging its corner), and click Make the Icon.

Create a Unique Flickr Address

If you want to share your Flickr photos with others, one way to do so is by creating a unique Flickr address and distributing it to those people with whom you want to share your photos. They can then simply type this address in their Web browser's address bar to view your photos on Flickr. They need not even be members of the site (although if they are members, they can take advantage of Flickr features such as leaving comments and so on).

The address begins with http://www.flickr.com/photos/; you then choose what text string, or "alias," should appear after the last slash. Choose your alias with care; once it has been selected, it cannot be changed.

---

① While signed into Flickr, click the You ▾ on the main page.

Note: *To sign in to Flickr, click the Sign In link in the upper right corner of the main Flickr page, type your Yahoo! ID (if it is not already displayed), type your password, and click Sign In.*

A menu appears.

② Click Your Account.

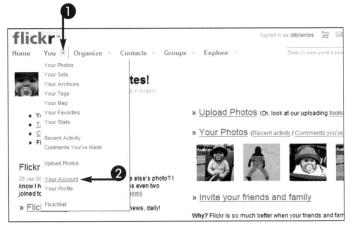

The Your Account page appears with the Personal Information tab displayed.

③ Click Create Your Own Memorable Flickr Web Address.

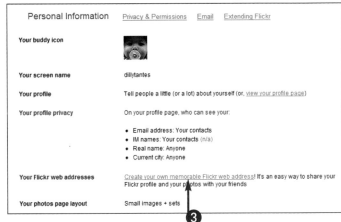

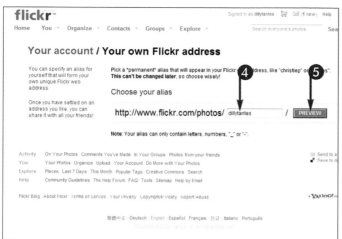

④ Type the alias you want to use.

⑤ Click Preview.

Note: *If another Flickr member is already using the alias you typed, you are notified of this and given the opportunity to enter a different alias.*

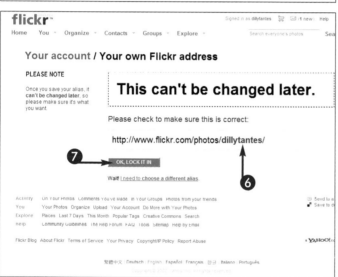

⑥ Verify that you typed the alias correctly.

⑦ Click OK, Lock It In.

Flickr locks in the alias you typed.

Did You Know?

In addition to creating a unique Web address with the alias you enter that enables others to view your photos, Flickr also automatically creates a unique Web address that provides direct access to your Flickr profile. You can share this address, which is in the form www.flickr.com/people/*youralias*, with others to allow them to visit your profile, even if they are not members of Flickr.

Invite Others to Flickr

If you want your friends and family to be able to leave comments about your photos and have access to other Flickr features, you can use Flickr to send them an e-mail invitation to join the site.

When someone accepts your invitation and joins Flickr, Flickr sends you an e-mail to notify you that the invitation has been accepted, and that person is automatically listed in your Flickr account as a contact. There are two types of contacts in Flickr: Friends and Family.

When someone is added to your Flickr account as a contact, not only can he or she view your photos, but you can easily view those of your contact; simply click the Photos from Your Contacts link that appears in your main Flickr screen.

---

1 While signed into Flickr, click Invite Your Friends and Family on the main page.

Note: *To sign in to Flickr, click the Sign In link in the upper right corner of the main Flickr page, type your Yahoo! ID (if it is not already displayed), type your password, and click Sign In.*

2 Type the e-mail address of a person you want to invite to Flickr.

3 Type the person's name.

4 Indicate whether the person is a friend, family, or both.

● Optionally, enter more contacts.

● Click Go Advanced to reach a screen where you can enter as many as 100 contacts.

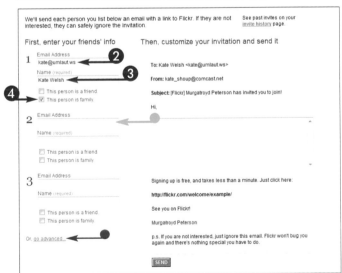

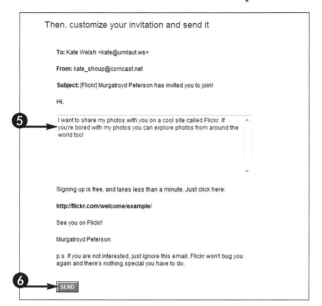

⑤ Optionally, customize the text included in the e-mail invitation.

⑥ Click Send.

Flickr sends the e-mail invitation to the designated recipients.

More Options!

In addition to adding contacts to your Flickr account by inviting them to join, you can also add existing Flickr members as contacts. To do so, position your mouse pointer over the member's buddy icon, click the ▼ that appears, and click Add *User Name* As a Contact in the resulting menu. Alternatively, display the member's profile page and click the Add *User Name* As a Contact link.

The photos you upload to Flickr can be visible to everyone on your site, visible to friends and family, visible to friends, or family, or visible to you only. By default, photos are visible to everyone.

Depending on a photo's subject matter, or on your own desire for privacy, you might want to limit who can view your images. One way to

do so is to change the default setting, as discussed in the tip on the next page. Note, however, that this setting applies only to any new photos you upload to Flickr; to change the privacy setting of any photos that are already on the site, you can use the Flickr Organizr, as outlined in these steps.

---

① While signed into Flickr, click Organize on the main page.

Note: *To sign in to Flickr, click the Sign In link in the upper right corner of the main Flickr page, type your Yahoo! ID (if it is not already displayed), type your password, and click Sign In.*

② Click a photo whose privacy settings you want to modify.

③ Drag the photo to the main workspace.

④ Repeat for any other photos whose settings you want to change.

⑤ Click the Permissions ▾.

⑥ Click Who Can See, Comment, Tag.

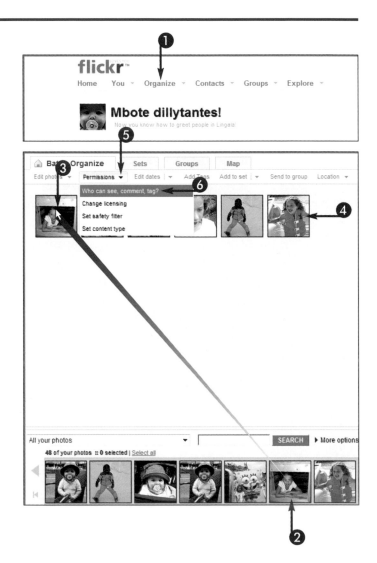

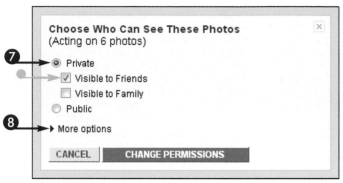

❼ Specify whether you want the image(s) to be private or public.

● If you chose Private, select whether the image(s) should be visible to friends, family, neither, or both.

❽ Click More Options.

❾ Specify who can comment on your image(s).

❿ Indicate who can add notes and tags to your photo(s).

⓫ Click Change Permissions.

Flickr saves the changes.

Note: *Click Thanks in the dialog box that appears to complete the operation.*

More Options!

To change the default privacy settings for all photos you upload to Flickr, click the You ▾ on the main Flickr page, click Your Account, click the Privacy & Permissions tab, and click the Edit link next to Who Will Be Able to See, Comment On, and Annotate Your Photos. Finally, adjust the settings as desired on the page that appears and click Save Settings.

Manage Viewer Comments

By default, any Flickr member can leave comments about your photos, and you can leave comments on any member's photos.

To leave a comment on someone else's photo, simply click the photo you want to comment on, type your comment in the space provided (assuming that the owner of the photo has enabled commenting by others), and click Post Comment.

If you do not want others to leave comments on your photos, you can change the default comments setting; you do so by following the steps in the preceding task, altering the Who Can Comment option shown in Step 9.

Assuming you do continue to allow comments, you can delete a comment you find offensive (outlined in this task), or block certain Flickr members from commenting (outlined in the tip).

---

1 While signed into Flickr, click Comments on the main page.

Note: *To sign in to Flickr, click the Sign In link in the upper right corner of the main Flickr page, type your Yahoo! ID (if it is not already displayed), type your password, and click Sign In.*

Note: *If no Comments link appears, it means no one has commented on any of your photos.*

The Recent Activity on Your Photos page appears.

- Click here to change the timeframe that constitutes "recent activity."

- Comments added in the timeframe specified appear here.

2 To delete the comment, click the photo to which it applies.

Bonjour, je m'appelle Heidi, et oui, je sais que je suis tres adorable!

Comments

murgatroydpeterson **says:**

What are you feeding this kid? Those are some serious fat rolls!!
Posted 9 minutes ago. (permalink | delete

③ Click Delete.

Delete a comment

Are you sure you want to delete this comment?

What are you feeding this kid? Those are some serious fat rolls!!

From murgatroydpeterson. 10 minutes ago.

☐ Block this user from commenting on your photos in the future.

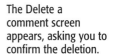

YES, DELETE IT

The Delete a comment screen appears, asking you to confirm the deletion.

④ Click Yes, Delete It.

Flickr deletes the comment.

TIP

More Options!

If a particular Flickr member repeatedly adds comments you find inappropriate, you can block all future comments from that member. To do so, follow the steps in this task to delete a comment from that member, but select the Block This User from Commenting on Your Photos in the Future check box in the Delete a Comment screen before you click Yes, Delete It in Step 4.

View Other People's Photos

More than a place to store your own images, Flickr is a community of photographers whose images can inspire and entertain you.

No doubt, photos that your contacts upload will serve this purpose; to view them, click Photos from Your Contacts or the Contacts link on the main Flickr page.

You are not limited to viewing your contacts' photos, however. You can also search for photos on Flickr by entering a keyword or the user name of a member in the Search box on the main Flickr page, clicking the down arrow next to the Search box, and then selecting the area of the site you want to search. To hone your results, you can use Flickr's Advanced Search tools, as outlined here.

① On the main Flickr page, click Search.

The Search page opens.

② Click Advanced Search.

The Advanced Search page opens.

③ Click the Search For ⏷ and select whether you want to search for all the words typed, any of the words typed, or the exact phrase.

④ Type a keyword or phrase.

⑤ Type any keywords or phrases you want to omit.

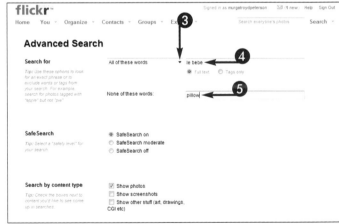

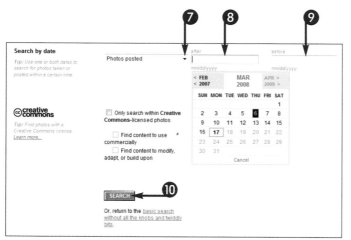

6 Click the scroll bar and drag downward.

7 To limit the results by date, click the Search By Date ▾ and choose Photos Posted or Photos Taken.

8 Click the After field and select the desired date from the calendar that appears.

9 Repeat Step 8 in the Before field.

10 Click Search.

Flickr returns a list of images that match your search criteria.

More Options!

You may have noticed the Safe Search options in the Advanced Search page. These options enable you to specify whether images that may contain objectionable content appear in your search results. By default, all of this type of content is hidden in searches; you can choose SafeSearch Moderate to apply a moderate-level filter, or SafeSearch Off to remove the SafeSearch filter.

Chapter 6

Keeping In Touch with E-mail, IM, and Internet Phone

For many people, the primary purpose of a computer is to keep in touch with others, be they friends, family members, or business associates. The Internet enables this in myriad ways, including e-mail, instant messaging, and Internet phone.

This chapter covers all three of these forms of communication, laying out the basics of using them as well as covering more advanced functions.

Specifically, you discover how to obtain a free e-mail account, use that account to send and receive messages, add contacts to the account, keep your messages organized, and block unsolicited e-mail messages, called *spam*.

You also explore downloading and installing Windows Live Messenger (one of the more popular instant-messaging programs on the Web), populate your Live Messenger contacts, and send and receive IMs. Finally, you find out how to download Skype, which is an Internet phone program, as well as add contacts to the program, and use the program to place calls of both the regular and conference variety.

Quick Tips

Many companies offer free Web-based e-mail accounts, which you can access using a Web browser, such as Internet Explorer, rather than a special e-mail program, such as Microsoft Outlook.

One advantage of using a Web-based e-mail account (aside from the fact that they are often free) is that it is accessible from any computer with an Internet connection. You might also create a Web-based e-mail account to have an alternate e-mail address for use when registering with various Web sites; this can help protect your main e-mail account from spammers.

A popular free Web-based e-mail service is Windows Live Hotmail. Here, you learn how to set up a Windows Live account, which gives you access to Hotmail, as well as to other online tools.

① Type **www.hotmail.com** in your Web browser's address bar.

② Click Sign Up.

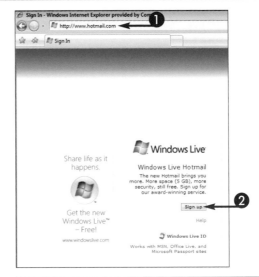

③ Under Windows Live Hotmail, click Get It.

Note: *If you want to use other Windows Live services, such as Windows Live Messenger (an IM program), click Get It under Windows Live Services (Including Hotmail).*

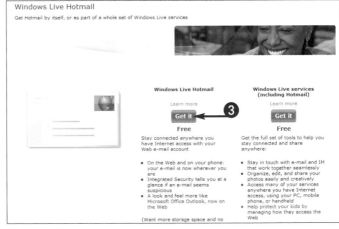

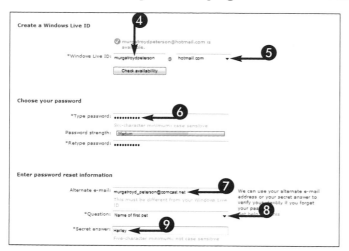

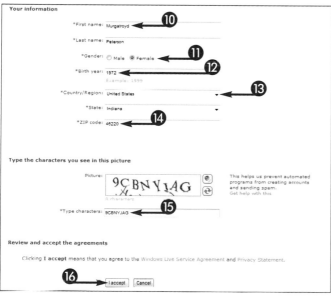

4 Type a user name.

5 Click the ⬇ and select hotmail.com.

Note: *You will be notified if the user name is not available.*

6 Type and re-type a password.

7 Type the address for an e-mail account you already use.

8 Click the Question ⬇ and select a security question.

9 Type the answer to the security question.

10 Type your first and last name.

11 Select your gender.

12 Type your birth year.

13 Click the Country and State ⬇ to specify where you live.

14 Type your ZIP code.

15 Type the characters shown.

16 Click I Accept to create your Windows Live account.

Attention!

After you click I Accept, Windows Live prompts you to select the type of Hotmail account you want — Classic or Full. If you simply need a quick and easy way to manage your e-mail, opt for Classic; the ensuing tasks in this chapter show this type of account. You can switch account types later by clicking Options in the main Hotmail page and clicking Try the Full Version.

To access your Hotmail account, you must enter your Windows Live login information. To do so, type **www.hotmail.com** in your Web browser's address bar. If your Windows Live ID appears in the ensuing screen, click it, click Sign In, type your password, and click Sign In again; if not, click Sign In with a Different Account and follow the on-screen instructions.

Messages sent to your Hotmail account appear in your Inbox. From there, you can open them, and then reply, forward, or delete them, as well as print them (assuming your computer is connected to a printer).

Of course, you are not limited to replying to messages; you can also start new message chains.

● The number of new messages in your Inbox appears here.

❶ To view mail you have received, click Inbox.

The Inbox opens.

● Unread messages appear in bold font.

❷ Click a message to open it.

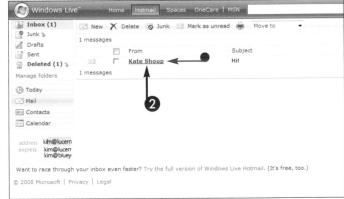

The message opens.

● Click Forward to forward the message to a third party.

● Click Delete to delete the message.

● Click the Print button to print the message.

❸ Click Reply.

Note: *If the message you received was sent to multiple people, you can reply to the sender only (Reply), or to the sender and all other recipients (Reply All).*

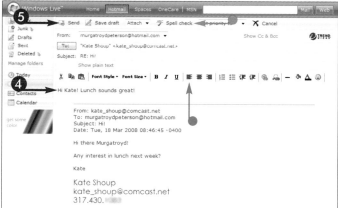

❹ Type your reply.

● Use these Edit tools to change the reply text's font, alignment, and other formatting.

● Click Spell Check to check the spelling in your reply.

❺ Click Send.

Hotmail sends your reply.

Attention!

To send a new message rather than reply to one you receive, click New. A blank message appears; enter the recipient's e-mail address in the To field (or click the To button and select a contact from the list that appears; to learn more about adding contacts to Hotmail, see the next task), type a subject in the Subject field, type your message text, and click Send.

Unless you are able to remember the e-mail address of every person you correspond with, you will want to use Hotmail's Contacts function to enter their contact information. That way, you can simply select your recipient from Contacts instead of having to remember his or her e-mail address when you want to send that person a message.

One way to populate your Hotmail Contacts is as follows: If you reply to a message sent by someone who is not in your Hotmail Contacts, Hotmail asks you if you want to add him or her to Contacts. If you do, click Add to Contacts. Another way to populate Hotmail Contacts is to enter a person's information manually, as covered in this task.

① **Click Contacts.**

The Contacts screen opens.

② **Click New.**

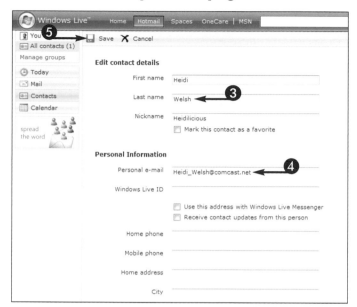

③ Type the contact's first and last name, and a nickname (if desired).

Note: *If you type a nickname, that is the name under which the contact will be filed.*

④ Type the contact's e-mail address.

Note: *At a minimum, you should type a contact's name and e-mail address, although you can enter as much information about a contact as you like. Scroll down for more information fields.*

⑤ Click Save.

Hotmail creates an entry for the contact.

More Options!

If you maintain a list of contacts using a program such as Outlook, you can import that list into Hotmail. To do so, first export your contacts from within the program to a file (see its Help information for details). Then click Options in the Hotmail Contacts screen, click Import Contacts under Customize Contacts, and follow the on-screen instructions to import the file you exported.

As you receive more and more messages in your Hotmail account, you may want to develop a method for keeping them organized. That way, in the event you need to find a message later, you will easily be able to do so.

One way to keep messages organized is by creating folders and filing your messages in

them. For example, you might create a folder for all messages you receive from a certain individual, or for all messages that relate to a particular project at work. You can then move all relevant messages from your Hotmail Inbox to that folder.

① **Click Manage Folders.**

② **Click New.**

The New Folder screen appears.

③ Type a name for the new folder.

④ Click Save.

● Hotmail creates a new folder with the name you specified.

Try This!

To move a message into a folder, select the check box next to the message (☐ changes to ☑), click the Move To ⊡, and select the folder from the list that appears. Hotmail removes the message from its current folder (for example, the Inbox) into the folder you chose.

Spam, which is computerized junk mail that typically advertises products and services ranging from unsavory to fraudulent, is more than just annoying — it represents an enormous time waster, and as such can be very costly.

You open yourself up to receiving spam when, for example, you register with sites or enter contests that require your e-mail address. But even if you keep your e-mail address private,

you may still receive spam sent to random addresses.

In this task, you learn to configure your Hotmail account to filter questionable messages. Filtered messages are moved to the Junk folder; it is recommended that you check this folder every few days in case messages you want to receive were placed there in error.

① Click Options.

The Options screen appears.

② Under Junk e-mail, click Filters and Reporting.

❸ Choose a junk e-mail filter level.

Low sends only the most obvious spam to the Junk folder. *Standard* sends most questionable messages to the Junk folder. *Exclusive* sends all messages to the Junk folder unless they are sent by people in Contacts, in your Safe Senders list, or from Hotmail.

❹ Choose when spam is deleted.

Choose *Later* to instruct Hotmail to move all spam to your Junk folder. Select *Immediately* to instruct Hotmail to delete spam immediately upon receipt.

Note: *This is not recommended; it prevents you from ensuring that a message is indeed spam.*

❺ Specify whether you want to report junk e-mail messages to Microsoft.

❻ Click Save.

More Options!

If a junk e-mail manages to bypass the Hotmail filter, you can flag it as spam, which instructs Hotmail to screen future messages from that sender's mail server. To do so, click its check box in your Inbox and then click Junk. Alternatively, block known spammers by clicking Safe and Blocked Senders in the Options screen, clicking Blocked Senders, typing the offending e-mail address, and clicking Add to List.

Download and Install Windows Live Messenger

Instant messaging (IM) enables two or more people to communicate in real time using typed text. One popular instant-messaging program is Windows Live Messenger.

The account you use for Windows Live Messenger, called your *Windows Live ID*, is the same account you use to take advantage of any other Windows Live service, such as Hotmail.

To download and install Windows Live Messenger, you must be logged in to the Windows Live site. To do so, type **http://home.live.com** and click Sign In. If your Windows Live ID appears in the ensuing screen, click it, click Sign In, type your password, and click Sign In again; if not, click Sign In with a Different Account and follow the on-screen instructions.

---

① After logging on to the Windows Live site, type **http://get.live. com/messenger/ overview** in your Web browser's address bar.

② Click Get It Free.

The Set Up Your Messenger page appears.

③ Review the default settings, deselecting any options you do not want.

④ Click Install.

A warning dialog box opens.

⑤ Click Run.

Another warning dialog box appears.

⑥ Click Run.

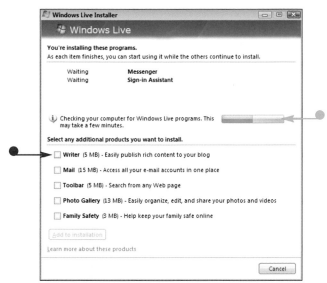

The Windows Live Installer opens.

● View the progress of the download/ installation operation here.

● Optionally, select additional programs to install.

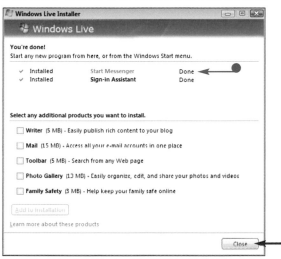

● Windows Live notifies you when the download/installation operation is complete.

⑦ Click Close.

Note: Depending on your computer's setup, Live Messenger may run automatically once it is installed. If not, launch it as you would any other program.

More Options!

If your computer runs Windows Vista, you can launch the Live Messenger download/installation operation right from your PC's Start menu. To do so, click the Start button, click All Programs, and click Windows Live Messenger. Windows Live Messenger starts, displaying the login screen; click Get a New Account. In the Windows Live Web page that appears, click Sign Up, and follow the on-screen instructions.

In order to use Windows Live Messenger to send and receive IMs, you must first add your contacts to the program.

You can enter extensive information about a contact, including his or her home and work addresses, phone numbers, e-mail addresses, mobile numbers, Web sites, birth date, the name of the contact's spouse or partner, and

so on. That said, all that is *required* to enter a contact into your Windows Live Message contacts list is the contact's name and e-mail address or mobile phone number.

When you add a contact, Live Messenger sends a message to the contact, inviting him or her to message with you.

---

① **In Windows Live Messenger, click the Add Contact button.**

The Add a Contact dialog box opens with the General screen displayed.

② **Type the contact's IM address.**

③ **Type a personal message to invite the contact to message with you.**

④ **Type a nickname.**

⑤ **Click to group the contact with co-workers, family, or friends.**

⑥ **Click Contact.**

⑦ **Type the contact's first, middle, and last name.**

⑧ **Type the contact's phone numbers.**

⑨ **Type the contact's email addresses.**

⑩ **Click to specify which e-mail address is the primary one.**

⑪ **If the contact uses an additional instant-messaging address, type it here.**

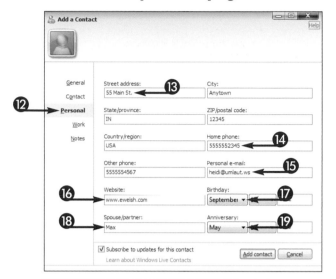

⑫ Click Personal.

⑬ Type the contact's home address.

⑭ Type the contact's personal phone numbers.

⑮ Type the contact's personal e-mail address.

⑯ If the contact maintains a Web site, type its URL here.

⑰ Enter the contact's birth date.

⑱ Type the name of the contact's spouse or partner, if applicable.

⑲ Enter the contact's anniversary, if applicable.

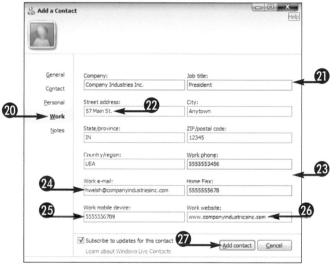

⑳ Click Work.

㉑ Type the name of the contact's company and the contact's job title.

㉒ Type the contact's work address.

㉓ Type the contact's work phone and fax numbers.

㉔ Type the contact's work e-mail address.

㉕ Type the contact's work mobile device number.

㉖ Type the URL of the company's Web site.

㉗ Click Add Contact.

TIP

Remove It!
To remove a contact from your list, right-click it and click Delete Contact. In the dialog box that opens, block the contact by clicking the Also Block This Contact check box to mark it. (Blocking a contact prevents that contact from seeing whether you are online and from contacting you.) Optionally, click Also Remove from My Hotmail Contacts check box. When you are finished, click Delete Contact.

Depending on the setup of your (and your recipient's) e-mail program, there may be a delay between the time you send an e-mail message and when it appears in your recipient's inbox. Even if the e-mail message arrives quickly, if your recipient is offline, there is no telling when he or she will actually see your message.

Instant-messaging programs such as Windows Live Messenger enable you to determine who among your contacts are currently online and running a compatible IM program, and then send and receive messages with those contacts with no delays.

You can also use Windows Live Messenger to send a text message to a mobile phone, place a phone call, and more. (For details, see the program's help information.)

RECEIVE AND RESPOND TO AN IM

- When someone sends you an IM, Windows displays it near the taskbar's Notifications Area.

1 Click the message.

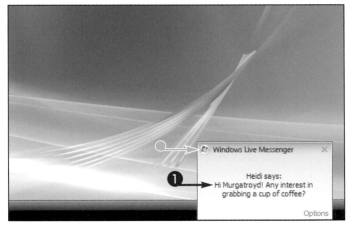

2 Type your reply.

3 Press Enter or click Send.

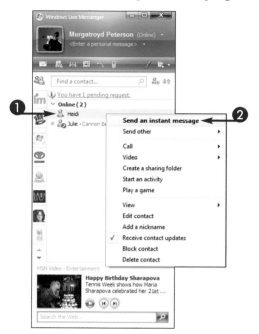

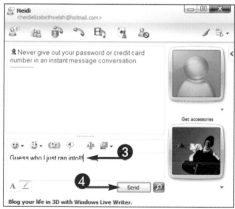

START A NEW IM THREAD

① In the Windows Live Messenger window, right-click the contact to whom you want to send an IM.

② Click Send an Instant Message.

③ Type your message.

④ Press Enter or click Send.

More Options!

In addition to typing text in an IM, you can also add *emoticons* to your messages — that is, special "faces" meant to convey a facial expression or emotion. Using emoticons can help prevent others from misinterpreting your messages. Also available are *winks*, which are animated greetings you can send to your contacts, and *nudges*, which cause the conversation window to vibrate.

In addition to communicating with others online via e-mail and IM, you can use your computer to place Internet phone calls to people anywhere in the world. One way to do so is by using a service called Skype.

You can use Skype free of charge to call other Skype users on their computers. Alternatively, you can place calls to ordinary or mobile phones for a fee.

To use Skype, you must first download it from the Skype Web site and install it on your computer, as outlined in this task. Once it is installed, you can launch the software just as you would any other program on your computer — for example, via the Start menu (PC) or the Finder (Mac).

① Type **www. skype.com** in your Web browser's address bar.

② Click Download Skype.

The download page opens.

A warning dialog box opens, asking whether you want to run or save the SkypeSetup file.

③ Click Run.

Another warning dialog box appears, asking you to confirm the operation.

④ Click Run.

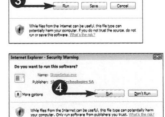

A Skype Install dialog box opens.

⑤ Click the Select Your Language ☑ and choose your language from the list that appears.

⑥ Select the Yes, I Have Read and Accept the Skype End User License Agreement and the Skype Privacy Statement check box.

⑦ Click Install.

Skype notifies you when the installation is complete.

⑧ Click Finish.

More Options!

The first time you launch Skype, you will be prompted to enter your name, the user name you want to use on Skype, and a password. You will also be prompted to accept the Skype user agreement, terms of service, and privacy statement. Do so and click Next; then type your e-mail address, select your country of residence from the drop-down list, enter your city, and click Sign In.

After you download and install Skype, you can begin adding contacts to the program. You can then phone those contacts with the click of a button instead of having to enter a number. You can access your Skype contacts by clicking the Contacts tab in the Skype program window.

One way to enter contacts is to do so manually, discussed in the tip on the next page. Alternatively, if you use Microsoft Outlook, Outlook Express, GMail, Hotmail, or Yahoo! Mail to manage contacts on your computer, then you can instruct Skype to determine who among the contacts you have entered into any of those programs are already using Skype. You can then import those entries into your Skype contacts.

① After launching Skype, click Tools.

Note: *You launch Skype just as you would any other program on your computer — for example, via the Start menu (PC) or the Finder (Mac).*

② Click Import Contacts.

The Import Contacts wizard starts.

③ Click the Start button.

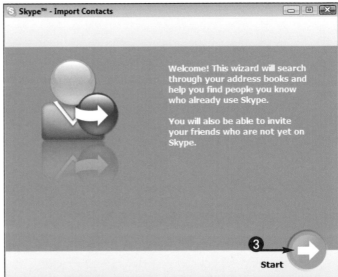

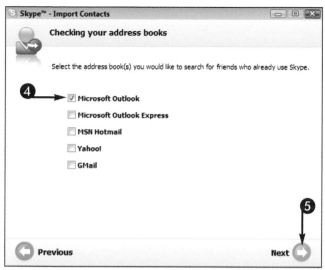

④ Select the check box next to the program you use to store contacts on your computer.

⑤ Click the Next button.

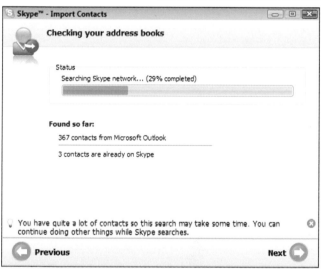

Skype checks your address book for contacts who are already Skype members.

More Options!

To add a contact manually, click Tools and click Add a Contact. In the Add a Contact screen, type a Skype name, full name, or e-mail address and click Find. Click the contact in the list that appears and click Add Skype Contact. If the person is not a Skype member, click Add an Ordinary Phone Number in the Add a Contact screen, type the contact's info, and click Add SkypeOut Contact.

If you have contacts in Microsoft Outlook, Outlook Express, GMail, Hotmail, or Yahoo! Mail who are not currently Skype members, then you will be prompted during the import operation to invite them to join the site and download the software. When they do, you will be able to phone them with Skype free of charge. (Note that even if someone does not join Skype, you can still use the service to call him or her, but doing so will involve a fee.)

Also, if you use Microsoft Outlook to manage contacts on your computer, you can instruct Skype to display all Outlook contacts that include phone numbers, regardless of whether those contacts are Skype members, in the Skype Contacts tab.

Skype lists contacts who are already Skype members.

⑥ Select the check box next to any Skype members whom you want to add to your Skype contacts.

⑦ Click the Add button.

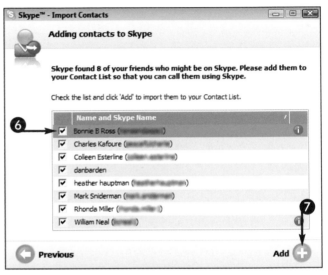

⑧ To invite a contact who is not a Skype member to join the site, select the check box next to his or her name.

● To invite all contacts, click Select All.

⑨ Click the Next button.

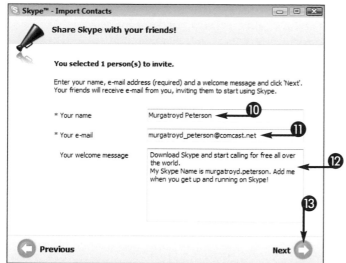

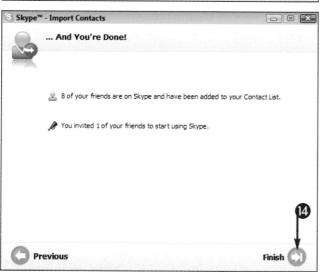

⑩ Type your name.

⑪ Type your e-mail address.

⑫ Optionally, edit the welcome message.

⑬ Click the Next button.

Skype summarizes the results of the import operation.

⑭ Click the Finish button.

More Options!

If your Outlook contacts do not appear in Skype, display them by clicking View and clicking Show Outlook Contacts. All Outlook contact entries that contain phone numbers will appear among your Skype contacts. To convert an Outlook contact to a Skype contact, right-click the entry in the Contacts tab and choose Add to Contacts. The Add a Contact screen opens; type the contact's info and click Add SkypeOut Contact.

When someone calls you on Skype, you hear a special techno sound effect. Simply click Answer in the Skype window to pick up.

In addition to receiving calls with Skype, you can place calls. Calls made to other Skype members on their computers are free; calls made to regular or mobile phones involve a fee. Before you make a fee-based call, you must purchase Skype Credit. Visit

www.skype.com, click Account, enter your Skype name and password, click Add Credit under SkypeOut, and follow the on-screen instructions.

To use Skype, you must have a microphone and speakers — preferably a combination microphone/speaker headset — attached to your computer.

① After launching Skype, click the Contacts tab.

Note: You launch Skype just as you would any other program on your computer — for example, via the Start menu (PC) or the Finder (Mac).

② Locate and click the entry for the person you want to call.

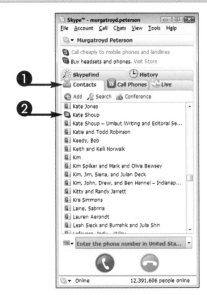

③ Click the Call button.

Skype places the call.

● The status of the call appears here.

● Once connected, the duration of the call appears here.

④ Click the End Call button to hang up.

Note: *If the person you want to call is not listed among your Skype contacts, click the Call Phones tab, select the country or region you are dialing, enter the phone number (including the area code), and click the Call button ( ).*

Did You Know?

If you have a Webcam installed on your computer, you can use it to make video calls on Skype. (Skype automatically detects the presence of a Web cam.) Assuming you are phoning another Skype member, video calls, like their audio counterparts, are free. You launch a video call by clicking the video button in the contact's entry in the Contacts tab or by clicking Start Video during a call.

Place a Conference Call

You are not limited to placing calls to a single person. You can also use Skype to make conference calls. At the time of this writing, Skype can conference as many as 26 people on a single call. Including multiple contacts in a single call involves the mere click of a button.

Note that you can include both Skype members and SkypeOut contacts in your conference call, although calling rates do apply in the latter case. If a party you want to call has not yet been added to your Skype contacts, you can simply type the person's number to add it to the conference.

---

1 After launching Skype, click the Contacts tab.

Note: *You launch Skype just as you would any other program on your computer — for example, via the Start menu (PC) or the Finder (Mac).*

2 Click Conference.

The Start a Skype Conference Call dialog box opens.

3 In the Choose Contacts list, click the entry for someone you want to include in the call.

4 Click Add.

● If a person you want to include is not listed among your Skype contacts, type his or her number here and click Add.

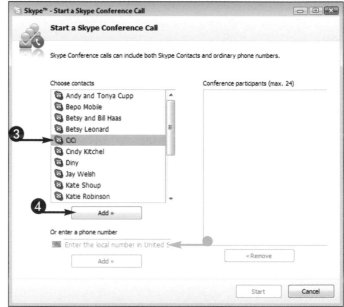

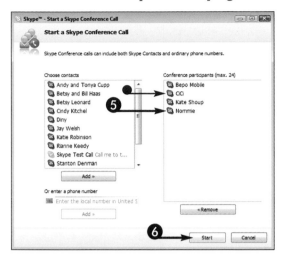

- The entry you selected in Steps 3 and 4 appears in the Conference Participants list.

⑤ Repeat Steps 3 and 4 to add more call participants.

Note: *To remove a participant from the Conference Participants list, click it and then click Remove.*

⑥ When all the necessary participants have been added, click Start.

Skype places the call.

- The status of each connection appears in the corresponding entry in the list.

⑦ Click the End Call button to hang up.

More Options!
If you use Internet Explorer, a special Skype button appears whenever you view a Web page that contains a phone number. You can click this button to dial the number using Skype. Alternatively, right-click the button to view more options, including one for adding the number to your Skype contacts.

Chapter

7

Connecting with Others Online

Recent years have seen the explosion of networking Web sites. These sites are designed to be communities where people with shared interests and activities can come together.

In general, these sites work by enabling members to post profiles. Members then link their profiles with the profiles of others to create networks of users, wherein communication can occur in various forms – comments, e-mails, IMs, and so on. Some networking sites also provide users with a platform for blogging, as well as for sharing photos, music, videos, and other media content.

As interest in these sites grows, so, too, do their numbers; some estimate that more

than 200 of these sites now exist worldwide. Among the most popular networking sites are MySpace and LinkedIn. The sites are similar in that they involve the creation of networks; they differ in that MySpace is geared toward facilitating social interaction of a more personal nature, whereas LinkedIn is intended as a way to facilitate connections among professionals – for example, to find potential clients, jobs, business opportunities, and so on.

This chapter merely scratches the surface of ways you can use these sites; for more information, see each site's help information.

Quick Tips

MySpace is designed to connect you not only with people you already know, but also with the people they know, and the people *they* know, and so on. You can use the site to share photos, blog posts, and more with your ever-growing network of contacts.

To enjoy all that MySpace offers as a forum for talking with friends online, meeting new friends, keeping in touch with your family,

networking, reconnecting with long-lost friends, and more, you must first create an account with the site.

After you create your account, MySpace gives you the opportunity to add a photo and invite your friends to join the site. Click Skip for Now; you will learn how to populate your profile in the next task.

① Type **www.myspace.com** in your Web browser's address bar.

② Click Sign Up.

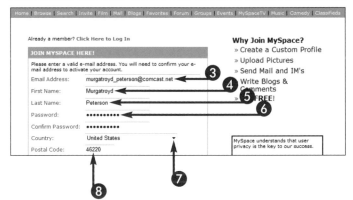

③ Type your e-mail address.

④ Type your first name.

⑤ Type your last name.

⑥ Type and retype the password you want to use to access the site.

⑦ Click the Country ▾ and select your country of residence.

⑧ Type your ZIP code.

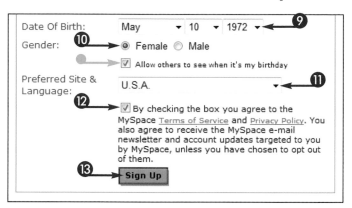

9 Enter your birth date.

● If you do not want others to see when it is your birthday, deselect this check box.

10 Select Male or Female to indicate your gender.

11 Click the Preferred Site & Language ▾ and select which version of MySpace you want to frequent.

12 Select this check box to agree to MySpace's terms and policies.

13 Click Sign Up.

14 Enter the text from the image.

Note: *This step helps prevent spam on MySpace by ensuring that only actual humans — rather than preprogrammed computers — are attempting to create accounts on the site.*

MySpace creates your account.

Verify Account

MySpace.com takes abuse seriously. Keeping MySpace.com free of abuse everyone.

Requiring users to correctly enter the text from the image below is one of

Please enter the text from the image in the field below.
The letters are not case-sensitive.
Do not type spaces between the numbers and letters.

TGB8HRMZ ◀— **14**

Continue to My Account

Important!
After you create your MySpace account, you will receive an e-mail message from MySpace containing a link to click in order to verify the account. Click the link as instructed to complete the account-creation process.

Populate Your MySpace Profile

When you create an account on MySpace, the site automatically generates your MySpace profile. Until you populate it with information about yourself, however, that profile will be fairly generic — consisting of your name, age, geographic location, and a few other tidbits.

You will increase the likelihood of making connections on MySpace if you populate your profile with information about yourself, such as your hobbies and interests.

In order to populate your profile, you must first log in to MySpace. To do so, type your e-mail address and password in the fields provided in the main MySpace page. When you do, MySpace directs you to your Hello page; from there, you can view and edit your profile, add photos, and more.

---

① In your MySpace Hello page, click Edit Profile.

The Profile Edit page appears with the Interests & Personality screen under the Personal Info tab displayed.

② Type an eye-catching headline for your profile.

③ Enter some text that describes you.

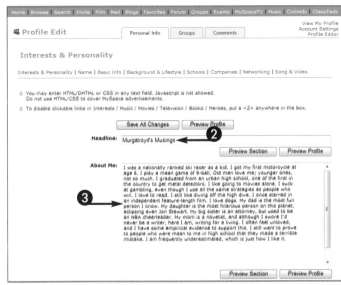

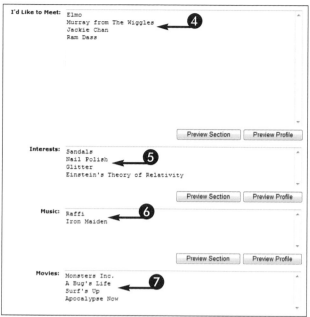

④ Type the names of some people you would like to meet.

⑤ Enter some of your interests.

⑥ Type the names of your favorite musicians, groups, albums, songs, or genres.

⑦ Type the names of your favorite movies.

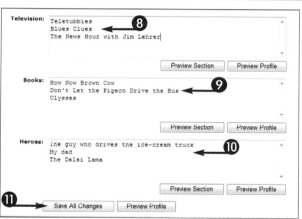

⑧ Type the names of your favorite TV shows.

⑨ Type the names of your favorite authors or books.

⑩ Type the names of your heroes.

⑪ Click Save All Changes.

MySpace saves the changes to your profile.

Note: To view your updated profile, click View My Profile in the upper right corner of the Profile Edit screen.

More Options!

This task demonstrates how to enter information about your interests and personality, but there are other categories of information you can add. To access these additional categories, click any of the links — Name, Basic Info, Background & Lifestyle, Schools, Companies, Networking, and Song & Video — along the top of the Profile Edit page and enter as much (or as little) information as you want.

In addition to adding text to populate your profile, you can add images. This can go a long way toward generating interest in your profile.

When you add images for the first time, MySpace places them in an album, called My Photos. You have the option of creating additional albums to better organize your photos. For more information, see MySpace's Help page.

If you add a single image, as outlined here, it will appear on your main profile page. If you add multiple images, you can designate which one should appear on your main page; visitors to your page can view the others by clicking Pics below your default image. (For help changing the default picture, see the tip at the end of this task.)

---

1 In your MySpace Hello page, click Upload.

Note: *To access your Hello page, log in to your account by typing your e-mail address and password in the fields provided in the main MySpace page. If you are already logged in, click the Home link in the upper left corner of the screen.*

The Upload Photos page appears.

2 In the Upload Photos page, click the folder containing the photo(s) you want to upload.

3 Select the check box for the photo(s) you want to upload.

● If an image needs to be rotated, position your mouse pointer over it and then click either the ↻ or the ↺ that appears.

4 Click Upload.

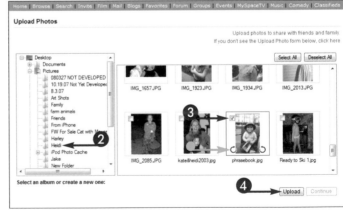

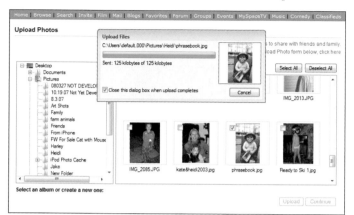

A dialog box
indicating the
progress of the
upload appears.

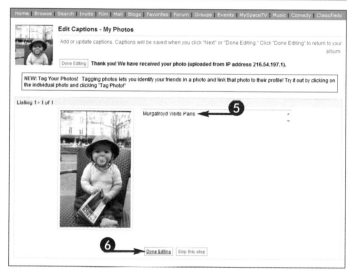

The Edit Captions –
My Photos page
appears.

⑤ Optionally, type a
caption for the photo.

⑥ Click Done Editing.

MySpace applies your
edits.

Note: *To return to the Hello
screen, click the Home link in
the upper left corner of the
screen.*

More Options!

To set a new default image, first add the desired image by following the steps in this
task. Then, on your MySpace Hello page, click the Edit link below your current
default image. Click the album containing the photo you want to use as the default,
and then click the photo itself. Finally, click Set As Default in the screen that appears.
When prompted, click OK to confirm the change.

Scan for Friends on MySpace

If you use Hotmail, Gmail, AOL Mail, or Yahoo! to send and receive e-mails, you can instruct MySpace to scan your e-mail service address book for other MySpace members. If it detects existing members among your contacts, MySpace gives you the opportunity to send each one a Friend Request. If your contact accepts your request, a link to his or her page will appear on your page.

You can also instruct MySpace to invite non-members in your address book to join the site. You will be prompted to do so immediately after sending Friend Requests to existing members. If you decide to wait, you can invite others to join the site at a later time; see this task's tip for more information.

① While logged in to MySpace, click Invite.

Note: To log in to MySpace, type your e-mail address and password in the fields provided in the main MySpace page.

The Find & Invite Your Friends to MySpace page appears with the Find Your Friends on MySpace tab displayed.

② Select the e-mail service you use.

③ Type your e-mail user name.

④ Type your password.

Note: The precise steps here may vary depending on which e-mail service you choose.

⑤ Click Find Friends.

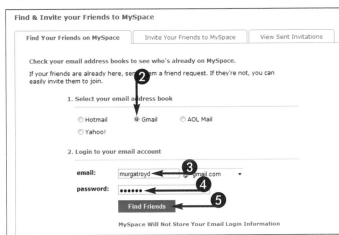

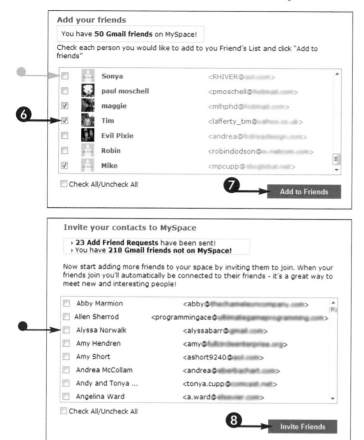

Add your friends

You have **50 Gmail friends** on MySpace!

Check each person you would like to add to you Friend's List and click "Add to friends"

☐		Sonya	<RHIVER@ aol.com>
☐		paul moschell	<pmoschell@ hotmail.com>
☑		maggie	<mlhphd@ hotmail.com>
☑		Tim	<lafferty_tim@ yahoo.co.uk>
☐		Evil Pixie	<andrea@ kidreadesign.com>
☐		Robin	<robindodson@ me.metcom.com>
☑		Mike	<mpcupp@ sbcglobal.net>

☐ Check All/Uncheck All

⑦ **Add to Friends**

Invite your contacts to MySpace

▸ **23 Add Friend Requests** have been sent!
▸ You have **218 Gmail friends not on MySpace!**

Now start adding more friends to your space by inviting them to join. When your friends join you'll automatically be connected to their friends - it's a great way to meet new and interesting people!

☐	Abby Marmion	<abby@ thechameleoncompany.com>
☐	Allen Sherrod	<programmingace@ ultimategameprogramming.com>
☐	Alyssa Norwalk	<alyssabarr@ gmail.com>
☐	Amy Hendren	<amy@ fullordeenterprise.org>
☐	Amy Short	<ashort9240@ aol.com>
☐	Andrea McCollam	<andrea@ eberbachart.com>
☐	Andy and Tonya ...	<tonya.cupp@ comcast.net>
☐	Angelina Ward	<a.ward@ elsevier.com>

☐ Check All/Uncheck All

⑧ **Invite Friends**

MySpace scans your e-mail address book for existing MySpace members.

● Any MySpace members whose e-mail addresses appear in your address book are listed here.

⑥ Select the check box next to each person you want to add to your Friends list.

⑦ Click Add to Friends.

MySpace sends a Friend Request to each person you checked in Step 6.

● MySpace gives you the option to invite people in your address book who are not currently members to join the site.

⑧ If you do not want to invite others to join the site, click Skip This Step.

More Options!

If you want to invite others to join MySpace at a later time, simply click the Invite link at the top of the MySpace page, click the Invite Your Friends to MySpace tab at the top of the screen that appears, and enter the desired addresses manually and click Send Invitation. Alternatively, instruct MySpace to scan your address book, and then follow the on-screen instructions.

Search for MySpace Members

With literally hundreds of millions of members, MySpace is great for finding long-lost friends. You can search the site to locate others with whom you have lost contact.

If you find someone you know on the site, you can send a Friend Request to him or her via e-mail. If your contact accepts your request, a link to his or her page will appear on your page.

In addition, you will be able to leave comments on your friend's page, among other things.

If you receive a Friend Request e-mail from someone else, you can accept or reject the request by clicking the link in the e-mail, selecting the check box next to the request in the screen that appears, and clicking Approve or Deny.

---

① While logged in to MySpace, type the name of the person you want to find on MySpace.

Note: To log in to MySpace, type your e-mail address and password in the fields provided in the main MySpace page.

② Click the ▼ and select People.

③ Click Search.

MySpace returns a list of profiles that match the text you typed.

④ If one of the profiles looks like it might be your friend's, click View Profile.

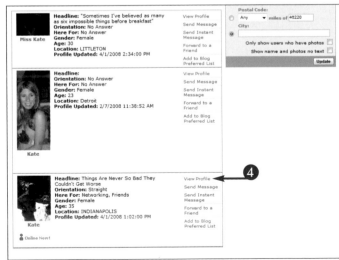

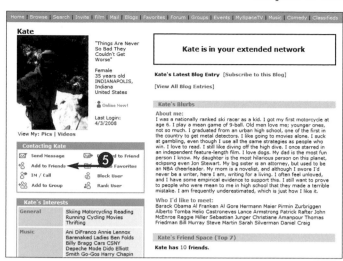

MySpace displays the profile.

5 Click Add to Friends.

The Add to Friends screen appears.

6 Type a personal message.

7 Optionally, select the Show My Full Name in This Friend Request check box.

● If your full name as it appears on MySpace is different from the name your friend knows (for example, if your MySpace name is your married name but your friend knows you by your maiden name), click Edit to change how your name appears in your Friend Request.

8 Click Add to Friends.

More Options!

To add a comment to a friend's page, click Add Comment in the Friends Comments area of your friend's profile. Type your comment and click Post a Comment in the screen that appears; then click Post a Comment again to confirm. Your comment will appear on your friend's profile, and your friend will receive an e-mail message indicating that a comment has been added to his or her profile.

Make Your MySpace Profile Private

MySpace is, at its core, a public space, designed to enable you to express yourself, connect with old friends, and even make new ones. For some, this type of exposure is part of the fun. Others, however, are more concerned with privacy.

For this reason, MySpace enables you to make your profile private — visible only to you and to anyone you have added as a MySpace friend. In addition, you can disable the Online Now status icon that appears on your profile whenever you are logged on to MySpace to prevent other users from detecting when you are on the site and when you are not.

---

1 In your MySpace Hello page, click Settings.

Note: To access your Hello page, log in to your account by typing your e-mail address and password in the fields provided in the main MySpace page. If you are already logged in, click the Home link in the upper left corner of the screen.

The Settings: Account screen appears.

2 Click Privacy.

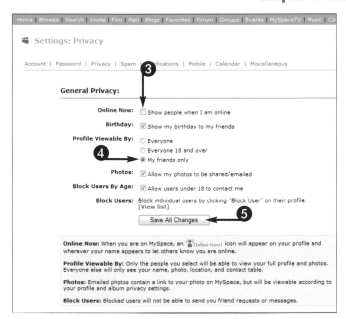

The Settings: Privacy screen appears.

③ Deselect this check box to prevent others from detecting when you are online.

④ Select My Friends Only to limit viewing of your page to your MySpace friends only.

⑤ Click Save All Changes.

● MySpace confirms that your privacy settings have been changed.

Important!

If a MySpace user makes you uncomfortable, you can prevent that user from contacting you by blocking him or her. To do so, visit the user's MySpace page, click Block User under the profile picture, and click OK. If you feel the user is a threat to you, notify the proper authorities; additionally, report the user to MySpace (click Contact MySpace at the bottom of any page on the site).

Join LinkedIn

With more than 20,000,000 members who work in some 150 industries all over the world, LinkedIn is an excellent networking tool for professionals interested both in maintaining their existing professional relationships and in forging new ones.

When you join LinkedIn, you create a profile that acts as an online resume, summarizing your professional experience and accomplishments. This profile helps others on the site locate you, whether they be former or current colleagues, clients, or partners.

You can link your profile with the profile of others, thereby expanding your own network. Specifically, your network includes your direct connections, their connections, and *their* connections.

---

① Type **www.linkedin.com** in your Web browser's address bar.

② Click Join Now.

The LinkedIn signup page appears.

③ Type your first name.

④ Type your last name.

⑤ Type your e-mail address.

⑥ Type and retype a password.

⑦ Click the Country ⊡ and select your country of residence.

⑧ Type your ZIP code.

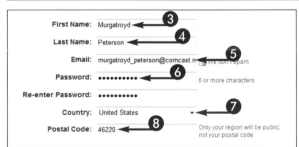

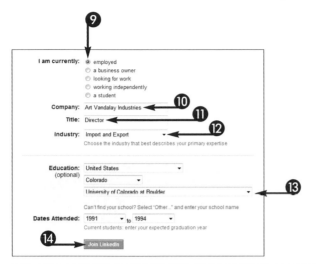

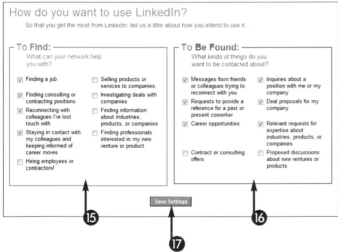

9 Indicate your current employment status.

Note: *The employment-related options may change depending on what you select in Step 9.*

10 Type your company's name.

11 Type your job title.

12 Click the Industry ▼ and select your industry.

13 Optionally, add information about your education.

14 Click Join LinkedIn.

15 Select check boxes to indicate how you want to use your network.

16 Select check boxes to indicate what kinds of things you want to be contacted about.

17 Click Save Settings.

Important!

After you create your LinkedIn account, you will receive an e-mail message from LinkedIn containing a link to click in order to verify the account. Click the link as instructed; you are automatically directed to a special confirmation page on LinkedIn; click Confirm to complete the account-creation process.

Populate Your LinkedIn Profile

When you create an account on LinkedIn, the site automatically generates your LinkedIn profile, which contains the information about yourself that you supplied during the account-creation process.

You will increase the likelihood of making connections on LinkedIn if you populate your profile with additional information about yourself.

This task covers adding information about previous jobs you have held to your LinkedIn profile. To enter other information into your profile, such as a summary of your work experience, additional information about your schooling, honors and awards you have received, or perhaps a photo, simply click the relevant link in the Edit My Profile tab shown in this task.

---

① In your LinkedIn home page, click the ⊞ next to Profile (⊞ changes to ⊟).

Note: *To access your LinkedIn home page, you must log in to the site. To do so, click Sign In on the main LinkedIn page and type your e-mail address and password in the fields provided.*

② Click Edit My Profile.

The Profile page appears with the Edit My Profile tab displayed.

③ Click Add Position.

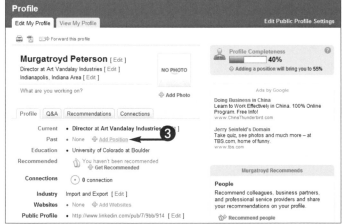

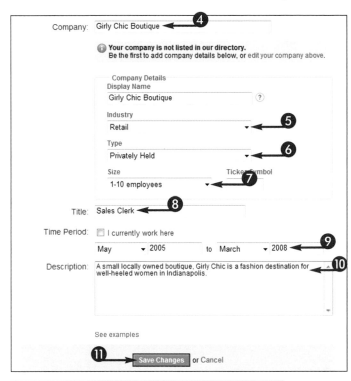

④ Type the company name.

Note: *If the company you entered is not in the LinkedIn directory, you will be prompted to add more information about the company.*

⑤ Click the Industry ⊡ and select the appropriate industry.

⑥ Click the Type ⊡ and select the company type.

⑦ Click the Size ⊡ and select the number of employees.

⑧ Enter your job title.

⑨ Enter the time period during which you held the position.

⑩ Describe the company or the position.

⑪ Click Save Changes.

● LinkedIn updates your profile.

Murgatroyd Peterson [Edit]
Director at Art Vandalay Industries [Edit]   NO PHOTO
Indianapolis, Indiana Area [Edit]

What are you working on?   ⊕ Add Photo

| Profile | Q&A | Recommendations | Connections |

Current   • **Director at Art Vandalay Industries** [Edit]
Past   • Sales Clerk at Girly Chic Boutique
Education • University of Colorado at Boulder

More Options!

To add a photo to your profile, click Add Photo in the Edit My Profile tab. Then, in the Add Photo screen, click Browse, locate and select the photo you want to include, click Open, and click Upload Photo. When prompted, crop your photo to best effect and then click Save Photo. Finally, indicate who you want to be able to see your photo, and click Save Settings.

Scan for Contacts on LinkedIn

If you use Gmail, AOL Mail, Yahoo! Mail, Apple Mail, or Microsoft Outlook to send and receive e-mails and manage contacts on your computer, you can instruct LinkedIn to upload your contacts to the site as well as scan your address book for other LinkedIn members.

If it detects existing members among your contacts, LinkedIn gives you the opportunity

to invite each one to link to your profile. If your contact accepts your request, he or she will appear among your LinkedIn connections.

This task shows you how to scan a Microsoft Outlook address book; if you use a different e-mail program, simply follow LinkedIn's on-screen instructions to scan it for existing members.

---

① In your LinkedIn home page, click Find next to Address Book Contacts.

Note: *To access your LinkedIn home page, you must log in to the site. To do so, click Sign In on the main LinkedIn page and type your e-mail address and password in the fields provided.*

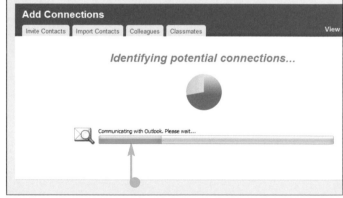

LinkedIn scans your address book for potential connections.

● The progress of the scan appears here.

LinkedIn uploads your contacts to the site.

- The progress of the upload appears here.

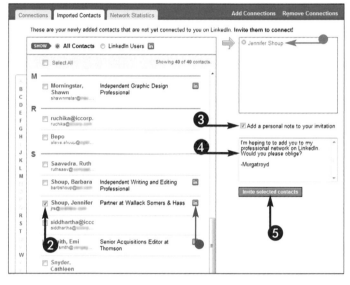

Your contacts appear in the Imported Contacts tab.

- This icon (in) indicates that a contact is a member of LinkedIn.

② Select the check box next to the name of a person whom you want to invite to connect.

- The person's name appears here.

③ Select this check box to add a personal note to your invitation.

④ Type your personal note.

⑤ Click Invite Selected Contacts.

LinkedIn sends an e-mail message to the selected contacts, inviting them to connect with you.

More Options!

Another way to invite others to connect with you on LinkedIn is to click Add Connections on your LinkedIn home page. In the screen that appears, type your recipient's first name, last name, and e-mail address, and then click Send Invitations. If the person is not already a LinkedIn member, he or she is given the opportunity to join the site.

With more than 20,000,000 professionals on the site, Linked In is great for tracking down former colleagues and schoolmates and long-lost friends. You can search the site to locate others with whom you have lost contact. When you do, LinkedIn returns a list of profiles that match the criteria you entered.

If you find someone you know on the site, you can invite that person to become part of your network and link your profiles together. LinkedIn then sends an e-mail message to your contact, inviting him or her to accept your invitation.

Assuming your invitation is accepted, your profile becomes linked with that of your contact, and your network expands to include that person, plus his or her connections, plus all *their* connections.

---

1 While logged on to LinkedIn, click the ▾ in the upper right corner of the screen and choose People.

Note: *To log in to LinkedIn, click Sign In on the main LinkedIn page and type your e-mail address and password in the fields provided.*

2 Type the name of the person you are searching for.

LinkedIn returns a list of profiles that match the text you typed.

3 If one of the profiles looks like it might be the person you seek, click his or her name.

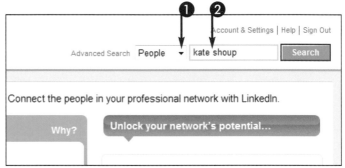

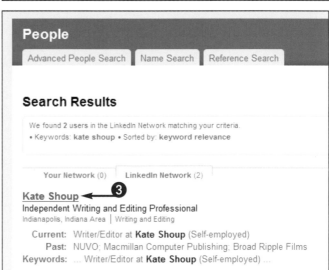

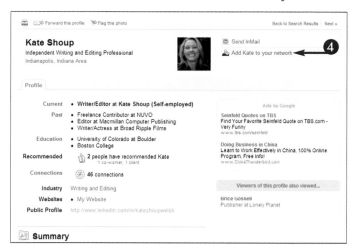

LinkedIn displays the profile.

④ Click Add *x* To Your Network.

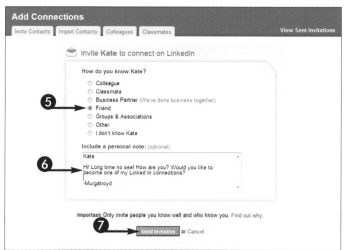

The Add Connections screen appears.

⑤ Indicate how you know the person.

Note: *Depending on your selection in Step 6, you may be prompted to provide more information, such as the name of the company where you were colleagues or the school you both attended.*

⑥ Optionally, type a personal note to accompany your invitation.

⑦ Click Send Invitation.

LinkedIn sends the invitation.

Important!

If someone else wants to connect to you via LinkedIn, he or she can send you an invitation. If you receive an invitation to connect with someone else on LinkedIn, you can accept or reject the request by clicking the link in the e-mail message containing the invitation and following the on-screen instructions.

Maximizing Your Success on eBay

At the time of this writing, eBay boasts more than 275 million members from around the globe who buy and sell goods and services of all kinds. If you want to join the fun, then this chapter is for you. It reveals how to set up your eBay account, and then delves into tips and tricks for successful bidding.

Specifically, you will discover how to research an item to determine if the price is right, avoid shady sellers, watch an item you are considering buying, enter your maximum bid, enter a last-second bid (called sniping) to up your chances of scoring a deal, and pay for your item.

If selling is your game, then read on; here you will find out how to create a simple item listing, how to jazz it up with eBay's Listing Designer tool, and how to use fonts and formatting to make your description pop. You will also learn the ins and outs of enhancing your listing's photos, as well as how to add a reserve price for those one-of-a-kind items. You will discover how to manage your auctions — those for which you are the seller as well as the ones for which you are the buyer — with My eBay.

Whether you are a buyer or a seller, the tasks in this chapter give you the edge on eBay!

Quick Tips

In order to buy or sell goods on eBay, you must first become a member, creating an account with the site. Membership is free.

Registering is simple: You provide your name, address, and other information, including a user name (this must be unique), password, and secret question. (If you forget your user name or password, eBay asks the secret question and, provided you supply the correct answer, sends you the information you need.)

After you complete the registration information, eBay sends you an e-mail that contains a link; you must click this link to activate your account. Once your account is active, you can bid on any item on the site, as well as list items of your own for sale.

① Type **www.ebay.com**.

② Click Register.

③ Type your first and last name.

④ Type your address.

⑤ Type your primary telephone number.

⑥ Type your e-mail address, and type it again to confirm it.

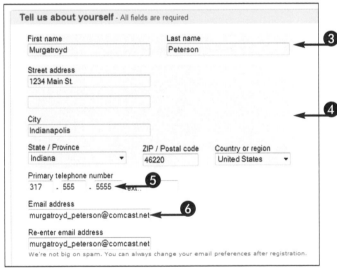

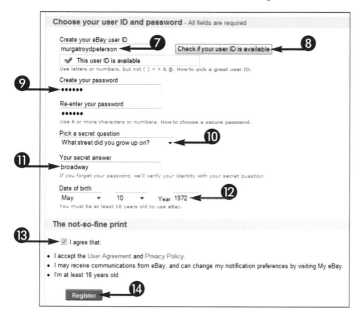

⑦ Type the user ID you want to use.

⑧ Click Check If Your User ID is available.

Note: *You may need to repeat Steps 8 and 9 until you find a unique user name.*

⑨ Type and retype the password you want to use.

⑩ Click the Pick a Secret Question ⏷ and select a question.

⑪ Type the answer to the secret question.

⑫ Enter your birthday.

⑬ Select the I Agree That check box.

Note: *Before you select this check box, take a moment to read the eBay user agreement and privacy policy.*

⑭ Click Register.

eBay creates your account and sends you an activation e-mail.

More Options!

Click My eBay in the top right corner of your screen to access your My eBay page. There, you view auctions you are watching, as well as ones you have bid on, won, or lost. Auctions for which you are the seller can also be viewed here. In addition, you can use My eBay to access tools for buyers and sellers, to change your account information, and more. See the last task in this chapter for more about My eBay.

Before you bid on an item, you should find out what similar items have sold for on eBay in the past to avoid bidding too much (or too little). To do so, perform a Completed Items search. This returns a list of auctions for items similar to the one you want to buy, indicating their final selling price. (Prices listed in green

indicate that the item sold; prices listed in red indicate that the item did not sell.)

Note that in addition to searching for completed items, you should consider expanding your research to other Internet resources, such as online stores.

① While signed in to eBay, click Advanced Search.

Note: To sign in, click the Sign In link at the top of the main eBay page and follow the on-screen instructions.

② Type a search keyword or phrase.

③ Select the Completed Listings Only check box.

④ Click Search.

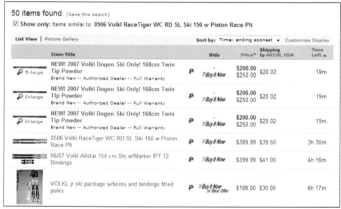

eBay returns a list of completed auctions that match your keyword or phrase.

● The selling price appears here.

⑤ If you see an item that is similar to what you want to buy, click View Similar Active Items in the listing.

eBay displays a list of similar items that are currently for sale.

More Options!

If no similar items are currently listed (or are listed at prices you feel are too high) you can save your search, and even instruct eBay to e-mail you when items that match the search parameters are listed for sale on the site. To do so, click Save This Search and follow the on-screen instructions. You can view saved searches from your My eBay page, discussed later in this chapter.

Check a Seller's Feedback

eBay recognizes the risk involved in participating in a marketplace where the seller and buyer may live on opposite sides of the globe. To help buyers bid with confidence, the site has established a feedback system, wherein buyers indicate whether their transaction was positive, negative, or neutral, and enter comments about their experience. You can avoid many bad experiences on eBay by researching the seller's feedback and dealing only with sellers who have a history of positive transactions.

eBay makes it easy to check a seller's feedback, displaying the seller's overall feedback rating as well as ratings that pertain to whether items are as they were described, communication, shipping time, and shipping and handling charges. You can also view specific comments from buyers.

① Click the entry for an item you want to view in more detail.

● View the seller's overall feedback rating here.

● This number indicates how many people have left feedback about the seller.

② Click the number indicating how many people have left feedback about the seller to view more detailed feedback information.

See a breakdown of the seller's positive, neutral, and negative feedback ratings here.

● View more detailed ratings here.

❸ Click the scrollbar and drag down.

❹ Read comments left by buyers about the seller and/or transaction.

Important!

eBay's feedback system relies on buyers and sellers taking the time to leave feedback in order for it to work, so you should make it a habit to do so after every transaction. You can leave feedback for transactions from your My eBay page. Click My eBay at the top of any eBay page, click the Feedback link under My Account, click the Leave Feedback button, and follow the on-screen instructions.

Track an Item Before You Bid

You can track items that interest you by using eBay's Watch This Item feature. For example, suppose you are searching for a particular item, and eBay has returned a very long list of matches. If you see an item on which you may want to bid — but you have not yet viewed all the results returned from your search — you can mark it by selecting Watch This Item, and then continue browsing the remaining results.

eBay gathers all items you are tracking, or watching, on one easy-to-access page in My eBay. On this page, you can see the item's number, title, current price, number of bids, time left in the auction, and the seller's user ID. For more about My eBay, see the last task in this chapter.

ADD AN ITEM TO YOUR WATCH LIST

1 While signed in to eBay, click the entry for an item you want to watch.

Note: To sign in, click the Sign In link at the top of the main eBay page and follow the on-screen instructions.

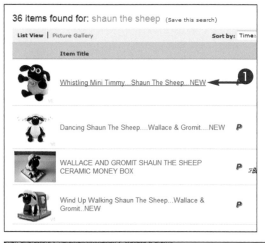

2 Click Watch This Item.

eBay tracks the item.

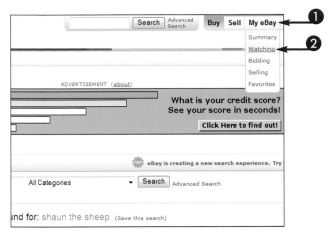

VIEW AN ITEM IN YOUR WATCH LIST

1 While signed in on eBay, position your mouse pointer over My eBay on any eBay page.

Note: *To sign in, click the Sign In link at the top of the main eBay page and follow the on-screen instructions.*

A list of options appears.

2 Click Watching.

The Buying: Watching page appears, displaying items you have asked eBay to track.

● To view the item listing in its own page, click its title.

Did You Know?
eBay e-mails you a daily list of tracked auctions scheduled to end within 36 hours. If you do not want to receive this e-mail list, go to My eBay, position your mouse pointer over the My Account link and choose Preferences, click Show All, click the Edit link alongside the Watched Item Ending Reminder entry under Buying Notifications, deselect the Email check box in the screen that appears, and click Save.

If an item you want to purchase is offered as a standard auction (rather than as a Buy It Now item, discussed in the tip on the next page), you can bid for it. The best bidding strategy is to tell eBay your maximum bid, and allow eBay's proxy bidding system to work its magic. This proxy bidding system places a bid on your behalf that is just high enough to outbid

the current high bidder. If someone later outbids you, eBay places *another* bid on your behalf — again, just high enough to outbid your challenger (assuming your maximum bid is high enough). This increases your chances of winning — and you may even wind up paying less than your maximum bid.

---

1 While signed in to eBay, click the entry for an item on which you want to bid.

Note: *To sign in, click the Sign In link at the top of the main eBay page and follow the on-screen instructions.*

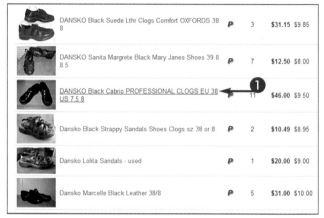

A page displaying more information about the item appears.

2 Type the maximum amount you are willing to pay for the item.

Note: *Bidding odd amounts increases the chances of winning, because most buyers bid using whole-dollar amounts. By bidding odd amounts, such as $13.01, you outbid those who bid a round-dollar $13.00.*

3 Click Place Bid.

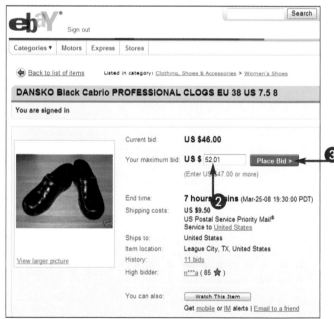

The Review and Confirm Bid page opens.

④ Click Confirm Bid.

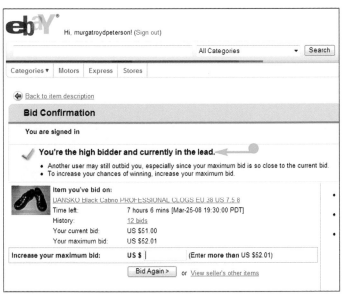

The Bid Confirmation screen appears.

● eBay informs you if you are the high bidder. Alternatively, if another bidder's maximum bid is higher than yours, you will be so informed.

More Options!
In addition to holding standard auctions to sell goods, sellers can employ a Dutch auction format (for selling multiple items), reserve auctions (where a minimum selling price is set; if this price is not reached in the bidding, the auction is null), or Buy It Now, which enables you to purchase an item at a set price.

Snipe to Win an Auction Near Its Close

You can increase your chances of winning an item by bidding in the last seconds of an auction, a strategy known as *sniping*.

One way to snipe is manually — that is, to take note of the auction's exact end time and place a bid on eBay just seconds before the end.

But what if the auction ends at an inconvenient time — such as when you are sleeping? In that case, you can use a sniping service to place your last-second bid, as outlined here. One such service is eSnipe; obtain an account with the site by visiting www.esnipe.com and clicking Join eSnipe Today.

---

① Type **www.esnipe.com** in your Web browser's address bar.

② Type your eSnipe user ID.

③ Type your password.

④ Click Log In to eSnipe.

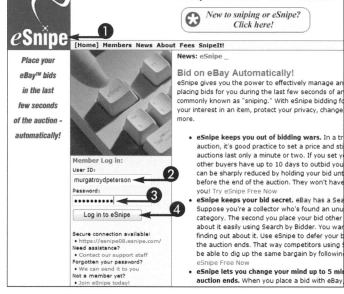

The eSnipe Bid Wizard launches.

⑤ Type the item number for the auction on which you want to bid.

Note: *Locate the item number in the upper right corner of the item's listing page on eBay. To ensure that you enter the item number correctly, consider copying it in the eBay window and pasting it in eSnipe.*

⑥ Click Next.

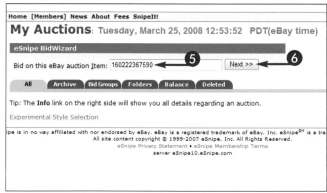

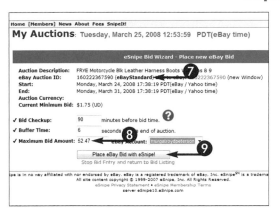

Home [Members] News About Fees SnipeIt!

My Auctions: Tuesday, March 25, 2008 12:53:59 PDT(eBay time)

eSnipe Bid Wizard - Place new eBay Bid

Auction Description: FRYE Motorcycle Blk Leather Harness Boots W... s 8 9
eBay Auction ID: 160222367590 **(eBayStandard)** .... 222367590 (new Window)
Start: Monday, March 24, 2008 17:38:19 PDT(eBay / Yahoo time)
End: Monday, March 31, 2008 17:38:19 PDT(eBay / Yahoo time)
Auction Currency:
Current Minimum Bid: $1.75 (UD)

✓ Bid Checkup: 90 minutes before bid time.
✓ Buffer Time: 6 seconds ..... e end of auction.
✓ Maximum Bid Amount: 52.47 .... eBay ccount: murgatroydpeterson

Place eBay Bid with eSnipe!
Stop Bid Entry and return to Bid Listing

...pe is in no way affiliated with nor endorsed by eBay. eBay is a registered trademark of eBay, Inc. eSnipe^SM is a trademar...
All site content copyright © 1999-2007 eSnipe, Inc. All Rights Reserved.
eSnipe Privacy Statement • eSnipe Membership Terms
server eSnipe10.eSnipe.com

⑦ Verify that the item number you typed was for the auction you intended.

⑧ Type your maximum bid amount.

⑨ Click Place eBay Bid with eSnipe.

Help   FAQ   Contact
Home [Members] News About Fees SnipeIt!

My Auctions: Tuesday, March 25, 2008 12:54:15 PDT(eBay time)   Maximize Size

eSnipe BidWizard

Bid on this eBay auction Item: Next >>

eSnipe Bid Wizard - eBay Bid Entry Results

eBay bid en... saved! Info link to review your bid entry. Your maximum bid amount is **$52.47** (eBay proxy bid). **eSnipe bid edit or cancel mu... e at least 5 minutes before bid time.**

All	Archive	Bid Groups	Folders	Balance	Deleted					
Select	Item Description	Status	Item #	Bid Amount	Quantity	Buffer	Auction Bid Time	Info		
☐	FRYE Motorcycle Blk Leather Harness Boots Womens 8 9	Ready to bid	160222367590	$52.47	1	6	03/31/2008 17:38:13	Info		

1

Delete   Move to >>   Archive ▼ Selected Items   ■ Auctions won with eSnipe   ■ Pending auctions   ■ Closed auctions

Tip: The **Info** link on the right side will show you all details regarding an auction.

Experimental Style Selection

● eSnipe saves your bid entry. At the designated time, it will bid on the eBay item on your behalf.

Remove It!

One advantage of using a sniping service such as eSnipe is that you can cancel an upcoming bid if you change your mind about purchasing the item — something you cannot do after bidding on eBay. (Note that you must do so at least five minutes before the auction closes.) To do so, select the check box next to the item in the My Auctions page and click Delete.

Pay Painlessly with PayPal

Congratulations! You won an auction. Your next step is to pay for the item. Your payment options will vary by seller. For example, some sellers accept personal checks; others require money orders. But the most common payment method on eBay is PayPal.

PayPal, a company that is owned by eBay, enables buyers to make online payments from their designated bank account or a credit card.

You can set up a PayPal account by visiting the PayPal Web site (www.paypal.com) and following the on-screen instructions.

Note that if you want to pay using PayPal, you should make sure that the seller of the item you want to buy accepts this form of payment *before* you bid. This information can be found in the item listing.

① After you win an auction or commit to purchase a Buy It Now item, click Pay Now.

② Select the PayPal payment option.

③ Click Continue.

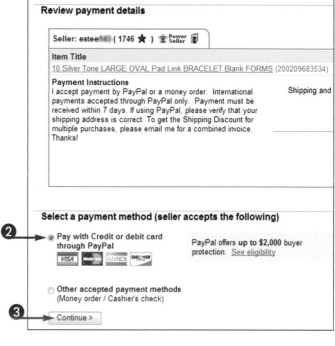

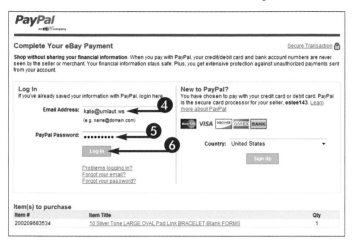

A Web browser window opens with the PayPal login page displayed.

④ Type your e-mail address.

⑤ Type your PayPal password.

⑥ Click Log In.

⑦ Confirm that the shipping address is correct.

⑧ Confirm that the price is accurate.

⑨ Click Pay.

PayPal sends your payment to the seller, and sends a confirmation e-mail message to you.

More Options!

In addition to expediting the purchase process, using PayPal can protect you if you do not receive your item or if it is not as described. In either case, PayPal can facilitate communication between you and the seller to resolve the problem. If that fails, you can enter a claim for reimbursement by PayPal. For more information, see PayPal's Web site.

Create a Simple Item Listing

Selling items on eBay can be as exciting — if not more so — than bidding on them; doing so can bring a great deal of satisfaction (not to mention extra cash).

Before you begin selling, take a moment to familiarize yourself with eBay's seller tools. To access them, position your mouse pointer over the Sell link on any eBay page and choose Seller Tools & eBay Stores.

eBay offers two options when you begin the listing process: Keep It Simple and Customize Your Listing. If you know your listing will be a fairly straightforward auction, and that you will accept PayPal as a payment method, opt for the first, as outlined here; for more customization choices, go with the second.

---

① While signed in to eBay, position your mouse pointer over the Sell link on any eBay page.

Note: To sign in, click the Sign In link at the top of the main eBay page and follow the on-screen instructions.

A list of options appears.

② Click Sell an Item.

③ Type a brief description of your item.

④ Select Keep It Simple.

⑤ Click Start Selling.

The Create Your Listing page appears.

⑥ Type a descriptive title for your item.

⑦ Click the category that best describes your item.

● If none of the categories shown is a good match, click Browsing Categories.

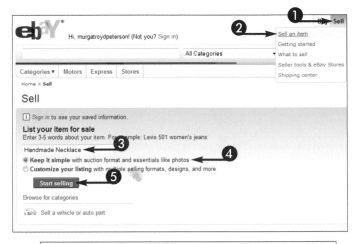

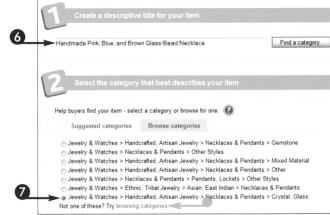

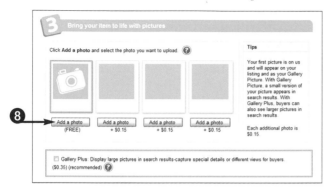

⑧ If you want to add a digital photo of the item to your listing (recommended), click Add a Photo.

An Add a Photo window appears.

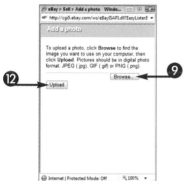

⑨ Click Browse.

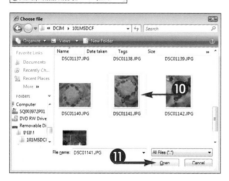

A Choose File dialog box opens.

⑩ Locate and select the photo you want displayed with your listing.

⑪ Click Open.

⑫ Click Upload.

eBay uploads the photo.

TIP

More Options!

You can add more photos by clicking the remaining Add a Photo buttons and selecting. For example, you might add photos that show certain aspects of the item for sale in greater detail. You should also include photos of any imperfections on the item — for example, scuff marks on shoes, small tears in fabric, creases on book spines, and so on.

continued

An important part of your item listing is the text description. When you write your description, attempt to describe the item as fully as possible, remembering to include any flaws the item might possess. Do not forget to check your spelling and grammar! Failing to spell correctly in your listing description and, especially, in your listing heading, can prevent interested buyers from finding your item.

Also important is determining how long your auction should last. Do you need to sell the item right away? Then a one-, three-, or five-day auction might be best. Want to allow time to attract more potential buyers? Then perhaps a seven- or ten-day auction would be preferable.

⑬ If your item is new, select the New check box.

⑭ Type a detailed description of your item.

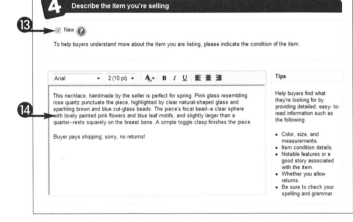

⑮ Type the desired start price.

⑯ Click the Lasting For ▾ and specify how long the auction should last.

⑰ Click the Shipping Destination ▾ and specify where you are willing to ship.

⑱ Click the Service ▾ and choose a shipping service.

⑲ Type the shipping cost, to be paid by the buyer.

⑳ Click Save and Preview.

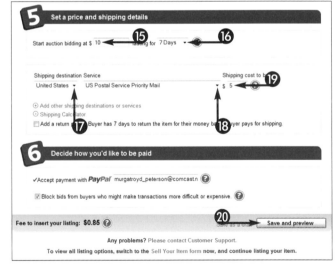

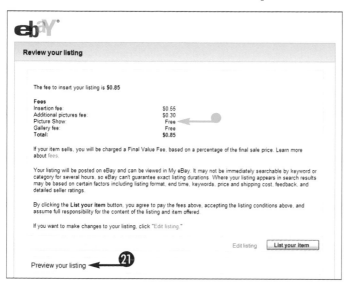

The Review Your Listing page appears.

● Review your fees here.

㉑ Click the scrollbar and drag downward to review the listing.

㉒ Click List Your Item.

eBay lists the item, and sends you a confirmation e-mail.

More Options!

If this is the first time you have sold an item, you will be prompted to specify how you want to pay fees assessed by eBay — with PayPal, credit or debit card, or from your bank account. Follow the on-screen prompts. To later change this setting, click My eBay, point to Account, choose My Account, click Change next to the Automatic Payment Method entry, and update the information.

Enliven Your Listing with Listing Designer

With millions of items for sale at any given moment, making yours stand out can be challenging. One approach is to use a Listing Designer theme to enliven your listing. Listing Designer themes set a default font and background color for your listing, making it a bit more eye-catching.

Listing Designer themes are organized into categories such as Special Events, Category Specific, Patterns/Textures, Holiday/Seasonal,

and so on; each category contains multiple themes from which to choose. You can also choose from various layouts to enhance the display of photos included with your listing.

In this task, you learn how to revise an existing listing to use Listing Designer. To use Listing Designer when creating a new listing, choose Customize Your Listing when you launch the listing-creation process.

---

1 In your listing entry on the My eBay: Selling page, click More Options.

Note: To open the My eBay: Selling page, position your mouse pointer over My eBay on any eBay page and choose Selling from the list of options that appears.

2 Click Revise.

The Edit Your Listing page appears.

3 Select the Add a Theme check box.

4 Click the Select Theme ⏷ and choose a theme category.

5 Select a design.

6 Click the Picture Layout ⏷ and choose the desired layout.

● A thumbnail preview of the design and layout appears.

7 When you are satisfied with the theme selections, scroll down and click Continue.

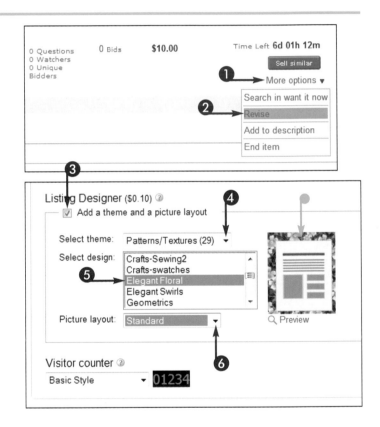

The Review Your Listing page opens.

8 Preview your listing.

9 If you are satisfied with the listing's appearance, scroll down and click Submit Revisions.

eBay makes the requested changes to your listing.

Important!

You must pay a small fee to use a Listing Designer theme. If you are considering using this feature — or any feature that involves additional eBay fees — you should consider whether this extra fee is worth it. This is especially so if your item is of the relatively inexpensive variety.

Maximize Descriptions with Fonts and Formatting

Although using Listing Designer (discussed in the previous task) does apply a specific font to your listing, it does not help to enliven your description text. Fortunately, eBay offers several formatting tools to enhance the appearance of the text. For example, you can change the text's font, its size, and its color; apply bold, italics, or underlining; and adjust the alignment and indentation. In addition, you can format your text as a bulleted list or a numbered list. You can, and should, take advantage of any (or all) of these formatting tools.

The description area acts like a word processing program; you click and drag over text to select it. In addition to applying formatting to selected text, you can also drag selected text to move it.

① In your listing entry on the My eBay: Selling page, click More Options.

Note: To open the My eBay: Selling page, position your mouse pointer over My eBay on any eBay page and choose Selling from the list of options that appears.

② Click Revise.

③ In the Edit Your Listing page, select the text you want to format.

④ Click to select a new font.

⑤ Click to select a font size.

⑥ Click to select a font color.

⑦ Click to apply bold, italics, or underlining.

⑧ Click to change the alignment.

● Optionally, click to run a spell-check.

⑨ Scroll down and click Continue.

Preview your listing Edit listing | Get help

This necklace, handmade by the sell spring!

Pink glass resembling rose quartz punctuate the piece, highlighted glass and sparkling brown and blue cut-glass beads. The piece's with lovely painted pink flowers and blue leaf motifs, and slightly la squarely on the breast bone. A simple toggle clasp finishes the pie

Buyer pays shipping; sorry, no returns!

The Review Your Listing page opens.

⑩ Preview your listing.

⑪ If you are satisfied with the listing's appearance, scroll down and click Submit Revisions.

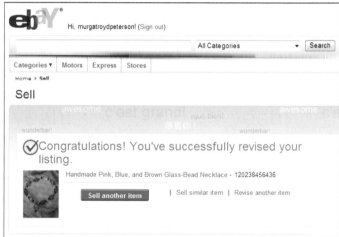

Hi, murgatroydpeterson! (Sign out)

| | All Categories | ▼ | Search |

Categories ▼ | Motors | Express | Stores

Home > Sell

Sell

⊘Congratulations! You've successfully revised your listing.

Handmade Pink, Blue, and Brown Glass-Bead Necklace - 120238456436

Sell another item | Sell similar item | Revise another item

eBay makes the requested changes to your listing.

More Options!

When composing your description, consider that most eBay shoppers do not read descriptions in their entirety. For this reason, you should include your key selling points near the top of the paragraph, saving any details for later in the block. Also consider formatting key terms in bold; this can help readers who are skimming your description grasp the basics.

eBay allows you to include one photo of your item free of charge, and additional images for a fee. Regardless of how many photos you include, using quality photos can attract both more bidders higher bids.

The effectiveness of a photo relates in large part to its composition. That is, haphazardly photographing your item in a box rather than,

say, polishing it and placing it in a pleasing environment will result in a less effective image.

That said, you can improve a good photo's effectiveness using image-editing software. For example, you can adjust its brightness and contrast, color, and other characteristics. This task demonstrates using Windows Photo Gallery to make a few simple fixes to your photos before you upload them to eBay.

① In Windows Photo Gallery, click the photo you want to include with your listing.

② Click Fix.

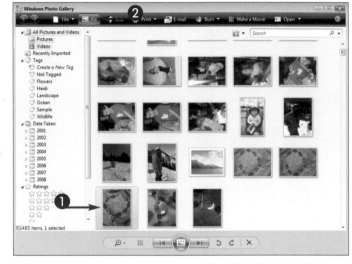

③ Click Auto Adjust.

Note: *Clicking Auto Adjust automatically applies the Adjust Exposure and Adjust Color tools.*

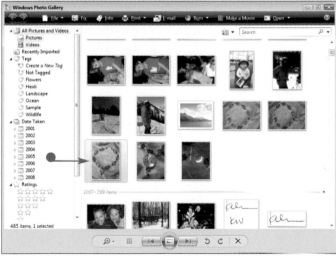

Windows Photo Gallery adjusts the photo.

● Click here to undo the changes.

● To save the changed version but keep the original intact, click File and choose Make a Copy. When you return to the gallery, you will be prompted to give the new version a name; do so and click Save.

④ To save the changes, click Back To Gallery.

● Windows Photo Gallery saves the edited version.

TIP

Important!

By default, many digital cameras take photos that are several megabytes in size. Uploading large images to your listing, however, can result in very slow loading of your listing page — especially for users with low-bandwidth connections like dial-up. To accommodate these users, try to change your camera settings to limit the size of your images. Alternatively, use image-editing software to reduce the size of your photos.

If your item is particularly valuable, or you simply do not want to sell it for less than a certain amount, you can assign a reserve price to it (for a small fee). This price, kept secret from bidders, represents the lowest price for which you are willing to sell the item.

When you assign a reserve price, the auction listing displays the text "Reserve Not Met"

until the bidding reaches the reserve price, at which point the text is removed. If the reserve price is not met before the auction ends, you are not obligated to sell the item to the highest bidder.

Be aware that setting a high reserve price can discourage prospective buyers from continuing to bid for the item.

---

① In your listing entry on the My eBay: Selling page, click More Options.

Note: *To open the My eBay: Selling page, position your mouse pointer over My eBay on any eBay page and choose Selling from the list of options that appears.*

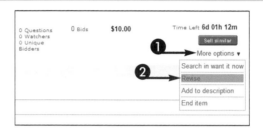

② Click Revise.

The Edit Your Listing page appears.

③ Next to Choose How You'd Like to Sell Your Item, click Add or Remove Options.

The Add or Remove Options dialog box appears.

④ Select the Reserve Price check box.

⑤ Click Save.

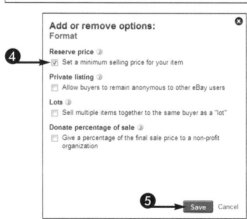

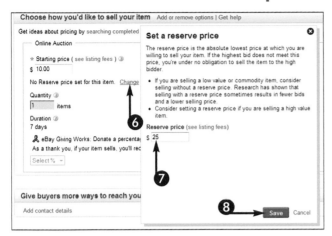

6 Next to No Reserve Price Is Set for This Item, click Change.

The Set a Reserve Price dialog box opens.

7 Type the price you want to set as the reserve.

8 Click Save.

9 Scroll down and click Continue.

The Review Your Listing page opens.

10 Preview your listing.

● Note the text that indicates that the reserve is not yet met.

11 Scroll down and click Submit Revisions.

More Options!

If your item typically sells for a particular price, you can use a feature called Buy It Now to give buyers the option of purchasing it immediately at a price that you set. To use Buy It Now, you must have a minimum feedback rating of 10. For more information about Buy It Now, including how to apply it to one of your own listings, see eBay's help information.

Manage Your Auctions with My eBay

My eBay makes it easy to manage your auctions, be they ones on which you are bidding, ones for which you are the seller, or ones you simply want to track in the event you want to participate.

In addition to enabling you to see the status of various auctions at a glance, My eBay enables you to read any e-mail messages from eBay to you, or messages sent to or from other eBay members — for example, for details about an item for sale.

My eBay is also the gateway to your account information, including your personal information, preferences, feedback, PayPal account information, and more.

---

① Position your mouse pointer over My eBay on any eBay page.

A list of options appears.

② Click Summary.

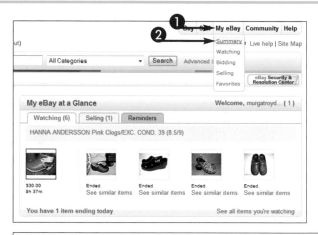

My eBay opens.

● Auctions that you are currently watching or bidding on are displayed by default.

③ Click Selling.

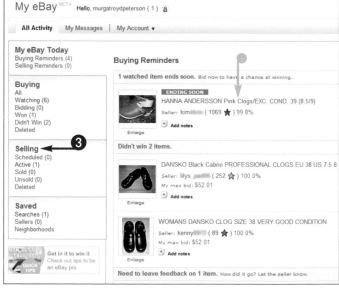

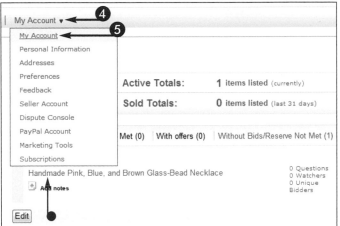

• Auctions for which you are the seller appear.

④ To view your account information, position your mouse pointer over My Account.

A list of options appears.

⑤ Click My Account.

My Account

eBay Live! registration is now open. Join us in Chicago June 19-21

My Seller Account Summary

Latest invoice amount: (View invoices)
Credits, payments and refunds applied to latest invoice: Show details
Amount due as of Mar-31-08:
New activity not applied to invoice:
Balance:

View recent account activity, fees, credits, payments & refunds.

eBay Seller Fees

PayPal is a convenient option for paying your eBay seller fees.

PayPal
MasterCard VISA DISCOVER BANK

Automatic PayPal Payments
The simplest way to pay your seller

Automatic payment method
Credit card
Credit card number: XXXX XXXX XXXX 5312

Last update:
2008-03-26 12:20:20.0

• My eBay displays your account information.

More Options!

My eBay enables you to enter feedback on multiple auctions from one location. To begin, click Leave Feedback in the Shortcuts section of any My eBay page. The screen that appears lists auctions for which you have not yet left feedback; click Positive, Neutral, or Negative for an auction listing, add comments, and click a star rating for each category. Repeat for any additional auctions, and then click Leave Feedback.

Chapter 9

Enjoying Media Content Online

In addition to being an excellent resource for information, the Internet is an incredible source of entertainment. Indeed, music, movies, and more are all available online with the mere click of a button.

Many online venues feature entertainment offerings — far too many to cover here. Instead, this chapter focuses on two major entertainment providers: the iTunes Store and YouTube.

Using the iTunes Store, you can quickly and easily preview and purchase music, movies, TV shows, music videos, audiobooks, games, and podcasts (which are typically available free of charge). You can also rent movies from the iTunes Store. You do not access the iTunes Store from your Web browser; instead, you must use Apple's proprietary iTunes software. You also use this software to play back any content you download from the iTunes Store.

In contrast, YouTube is a video-sharing Web site that you access from your Web browser. On YouTube, you can view video clips that have been uploaded by others, as well as share your own. Since its inception in 2005, YouTube has grown to host more than 70,000,000 videos ranging from clips produced by amateurs to content provided by major networks.

Quick Tips

One of the most common tools for previewing and purchasing media content online is iTunes. Specifically, you can use iTunes to preview and purchase (and, in some cases, rent) music, videos, and movies that are available from the iTunes Store. You can also use iTunes to download and listen to video and audio podcasts, as well as enjoy Internet radio and other Internet broadcasts.

Before you can use iTunes, you must download and install it. This operation involves stepping through a series of screens in order to specify your preferences. Note that in this task, these steps were performed using Internet Explorer 7 on a PC running Windows Vista; if you use a Mac, the steps will vary. Simply follow the on-screen prompts.

① Type **www.apple.com/itunes/download** in your Web browser's address bar.

   The Download iTunes page opens.

● System requirements for running iTunes appear here.

● To receive Apple's New Music Tuesday newsletter, select the E-mail Me New Music Tuesday check box.

● To receive Apple news, software updates, and so on, select the Keep Me Up to Date check box.

② Type your e-mail address.

③ Click Download iTunes Free.

   Your browser asks whether you want to run the iTunesSetup file.

④ Click Run.

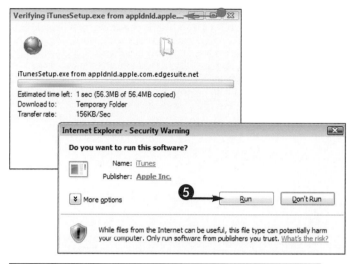

● Your computer downloads iTunesSetup.

❺ When the download is complete, your browser asks whether you want to run iTunes. Click Run.

Note: Although the browser asks whether you want to run iTunes, clicking Run in fact launches the iTunes installer. Only after the installer runs can you launch iTunes.

❻ The iTunes Installer starts. Click Next.

Attention!

From time to time, Apple updates its iTunes software to resolve bugs, add new features, and so on. To check whether you have the most recent version of the software, open the iTunes Help menu and choose Check for Updates. iTunes checks to see whether you have the most current version; if not, it steps you through the update process. (Note that you must be online to check for updates.)

As you step through the download and install process, you are given the opportunity to set various preferences. For example, you can specify whether you want to add shortcuts to iTunes and QuickTime on your desktop (more about QuickTime in the tip on this page), iTunes' default language, and the folder in which iTunes' program files are stored. You are also prompted to specify whether iTunes should warn you if it is not the default audio player. (To make iTunes the default player, open the Edit menu in iTunes and choose Preferences. In the dialog box that appears, click the Advanced tab, click General, and select the Use iTunes as the Default Player for Audio Files check box.)

iTunes Installer displays Apple's license agreement.

⑦ Click I Accept the Terms in the License Agreement.

⑧ Click Next.

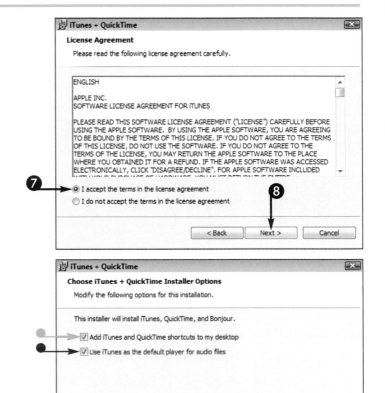

The Choose iTunes + QuickTime Installer Options screen appears.

● Optionally, select Add Desktop Shortcuts.

● Optionally, select Use iTunes as the Default Player for Audio Files.

● Optionally, click the Default iTunes Language ▾ and choose the desired language.

● Optionally, click Change and select the folder in which you want to save iTunes' program files.

⑨ Click Install.

The iTunes installer displays a progress dialog box, indicating the status of the installation process.

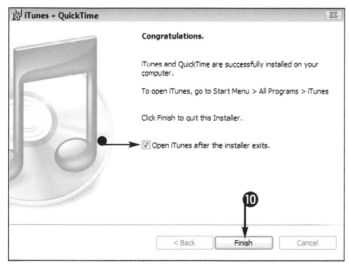

The program is installed.

● If you want to launch iTunes after exiting the installer, select Open iTunes After the Installer Exits.

⑩ Click Finish.

Did You Know?

When you run the iTunes installer, the latest version of QuickTime is installed on your computer. QuickTime plays a key role in iTunes' ability to play back media content. Also installed is Bonjour, a technology designed to automatically connect computers and smart devices. Bonjour works with iTunes to enable you to share music with others on your local network.

At Apple's online iTunes Store, you can find, preview, and purchase songs, albums, videos, television episodes, audio books, and games. In addition, you also have the option of renting some video content. The iTunes Store also offers some content free of charge — for example, the store offers a free music single each week, as well as free podcasts.

Although the iTunes Store is an online storefront, you do not access it with your Web browser as you do other e-commerce sites. Instead, you access the iTunes Store from within the iTunes program installed on your computer.

You do not need an iTunes account to visit the iTunes Store, but you do in order to purchase content from the store. See the next task for more information.

① In the iTunes window, click iTunes Store in the source list.

iTunes connects you to the iTunes Store.

● To search for content in the iTunes Store, type a keyword in the Search field.

● Click these buttons to move backward and forward through already viewed screens in the iTunes Store or to access the iTunes Store's main screen.

● Click the Browse button to open a special panel that enables you to browse iTunes Store content by categories such as genre, artist, and so on.

● Click these links for quick access to the various iTunes Store categories.

● Click the tabs in the New Releases section to access the latest music, movies, TV shows, and so on.

● Click these links to launch the iTunes Store's Browse and Search functions, access your account, buy iTunes gifts, redeem gift certificates, obtain support, and more.

More Options!

As you scroll down the iTunes Store's main screen, yet more options appear, including links to the top movie rentals, songs, albums, TV episodes, music videos, podcasts, audiobooks, and more. In addition, you will find links to staff favorites, free content, and a special "Just for You" section with quick access to content that is selected based on your previous purchases.

Although you do not need an account to visit the iTunes Store, you must create an Apple account if you intend to purchase content from the store.

The instructions here cover setting up an account for the U.S.-based iTunes Store. If your billing address is outside the United States, click the link above the license agreement and follow the on-screen instructions.

If you already have an Apple account — for example, if you created an Apple account at the Apple Store Web site — you can use the user name and password for that account to log on to the iTunes Store. Likewise, if you are an AOL user, your AOL user name and password can be used to log on to the iTunes Store.

① Click Store.

② Click Create Account.

③ Read the license agreement in the Create an Apple Account for the US iTunes Store screen.

④ Select I Have Read and Agree to the iTunes Terms and Conditions.

⑤ Click Continue.

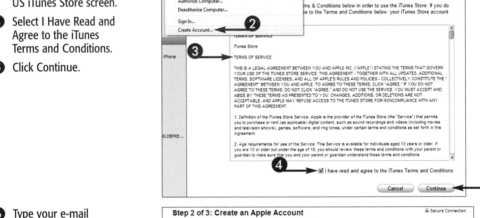

⑥ Type your e-mail address.

⑦ Type and retype the password you want to use.

⑧ Type a question and an answer (used to confirm your identity if you forget your password).

⑨ Select your birth month and date.

● Select this check box to receive news from the iTunes store.

● Select this check box to receive news from Apple.

⑩ Click Continue.

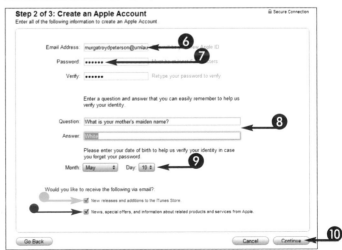

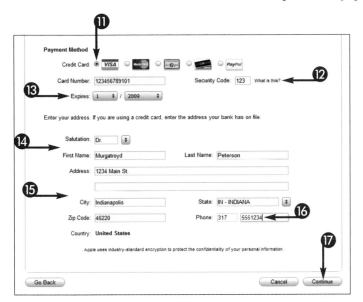

⑪ Choose the desired payment type (here, a credit card).

Note: *If you choose PayPal, the screen changes to include a different set of options. Simply follow the on-screen prompts.*

⑫ Type the credit-card's number and security code.

⑬ Select the card's expiration month and year.

⑭ Type your first and last name.

⑮ Type your address.

⑯ Type your phone number.

⑰ Click Continue.

Your Apple account is created.

⑱ Click Done.

Important!
Depending on your computer's settings, you may be automatically logged in to the iTunes store when you visit it. If not, you can log in manually by opening the Store menu and choosing Sign In. In the dialog box that appears, type your Apple ID and password and click Sign In. To sign out, open the Store menu and click Sign Out.

If you need to change your account information for the iTunes Store, you can easily do so. For example, if you move, or if your credit card expires, you need to change your address and/or payment information accordingly.

Alternatively, you can set certain preferences for your account. For example, you can create a nickname and perform other tasks.

In order to change your account settings, you must be logged in to the iTunes Store. To do so, open the Store menu and choose Sign In; in the dialog box that appears, type your Apple ID and password and click Sign In.

① While logged in to the iTunes Store, click Store.

② Click View My Account.

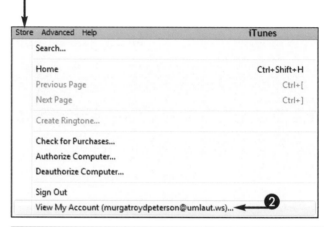

③ If prompted, type your Apple ID.

④ Type your password.

⑤ Click View Account.

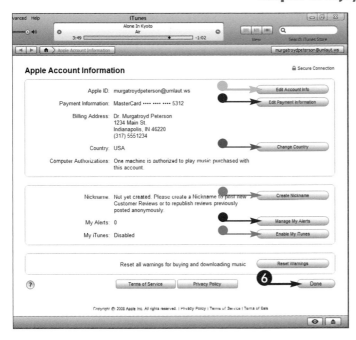

- In the Apple Account Information screen, click Edit Account Info to change your Apple ID, password, and newsletter settings.

- Click Edit Payment Information to change your payment type and card information.

- Click Change Country if your billing address has changed to a new country.

- Click Create Nickname to create a nickname for use when posting reviews.

- Click Manage My Alerts to specify whether the iTunes Store should send you e-mails when new content from artists whose work you have purchased before is released.

- Click Enable My iTunes to share your favorite content with others on Web sites you maintain, such as a blog or social-networking page.

6 Click Done.

Important!

Before you can use a computer to play content purchased from the iTunes Store, you must authorize that computer. To authorize a computer, click Store and click Authorize Computer. In the dialog box that appears, enter your Apple ID and password and click Authorize. If you later decide to sell or give away your computer, deauthorize it by clicking Store, choosing Deauthorize Computer, and following the on-screen prompts.

Locate Content in the iTunes Store

As of this writing, the iTunes Store catalog featured more than 6,000,000 songs — not to mention podcasts, audiobooks, TV shows, movies for rent or purchase, and games.

As great as it is to have such a wide selection of content, it can make finding the content you want a bit of a hassle. One approach is to simply click the various links available in the

iTunes Store and see where you land. A more targeted approach, however, is to use the iTunes Store's Browse feature. It enables you to pinpoint the content you want with just a few clicks of a mouse. You can also use the program's Search field to locate a particular item.

---

1 Click the Browse button.

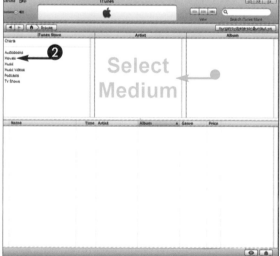

• The iTunes Store screen changes to include several panes, with the leftmost pane containing a list of the various iTunes Store content categories.

2 Click the desired content category (here, Movies).

● The iTunes Store displays a list of movie genres in the Genre pane.

Note: The panes that appear differ depending on what content category you choose. For example, choosing Movies results in only two panes appearing (iTunes Store and Genre), and choosing Music results in the five panes appearing (iTunes Store, Genre, Subgenre, Artist, and Album).

❸ Click a movie genre.

● The iTunes Store lists available movies in the selected genre.

More Options!

Another way to locate content is to type a keyword in the Search field in the upper-right corner of the iTunes Store screen; this displays a list of available items that contain the keyword or phrase you typed. Alternatively, try using the iTunes Store's Power Search feature, which you access by clicking the Power Search link in the Quick Links area of the main iTunes Store screen.

The iTunes Store enables you to preview content in its catalog before you buy. For example, you can listen to a 30-second preview of any song to determine whether it is indeed a song you want to buy.

If you decide to purchase content from the iTunes Store, the file containing that content is downloaded to your computer, where it will be saved in your iTunes library and in the Purchases playlist. If the download process is interrupted, it automatically resumes the next time you connect to the iTunes Store, at no extra charge to you. (If the download process does not resume automatically, open the Store menu and choose Check for Purchases, enter your Apple ID and password, and click Check.)

PREVIEW CONTENT

① After you locate the content you want to preview, click it.

② Click the Play button.

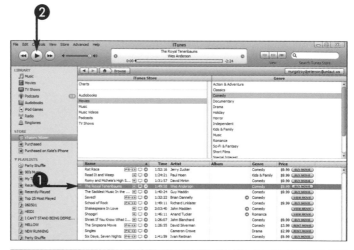

The preview (here, a movie) plays.

Note: *If the playback is jittery, you can adjust your computer's settings to load the entire preview before playing it. To do so, open the Edit menu, choose Preferences, click the Store tab in the iTunes dialog box that appears, select the Load Complete Preview Before Playing check box, and click OK.*

PURCHASE CONTENT

① Click the item you want to purchase.

② Click Buy *Content* to download the file to your computer.

Note: *If you are not signed in, or if your account setup requires you to enter a password to purchase content, the iTunes Store prompts you to enter your Apple ID and password.*

Note: *Depending on your account settings, the iTunes Store may prompt you to confirm the purchase. Click Buy.*

③ To view the progress of the download, click Downloads.

● The download status appears.

● Click Purchased to view items you have purchased from the iTunes Store.

Note: *To play an item, click it in the Purchased list and then click the Play button.*

Did You Know?

In addition to offering content for purchase, the iTunes Store also offers certain movies for rent. If a movie is available on iTunes for rent, it will feature a Rent Movie button; click it to download the movie to your computer. You have 30 days to start watching a rented movie, although once you begin viewing the movie, its availability expires after 24 hours.

Subscribe to a Podcast

A *podcast* — short for *iPod* and *broadcast* — is a digital media file that is distributed over the Internet. Typically, a podcast file contains an episode of a radio- or television-style show. Podcasts are typically free of charge.

You can download individual podcast episodes from the iTunes Store. If you find that you really like a podcast, you can subscribe to it. When you subscribe to a podcast, files for new episodes are downloaded automatically.

If you no longer want iTunes to automatically download new episodes of a podcast, you can unsubscribe from it. To do so, click Podcasts in the source list, click the podcast from which you want to unsubscribe, and click the Unsubscribe button at the bottom of the screen.

① In the main screen of the iTunes Store, click the Podcasts link.

② Locate the desired podcast.

● To preview a podcast before you subscribe, click Get Episode next to an episode that sounds interesting. iTunes downloads the episode; play it back by following the steps in the next task.

③ Click Subscribe.

An iTunes dialog box appears, asking you to confirm the subscription.

④ Click Subscribe.

iTunes subscribes you to the podcast and downloads the most recent podcast episode from the iTunes Store.

⑤ When the download is complete, click Podcasts in the source list.

● The podcast appears in the file list.

Did You Know?

If the podcast you want to subscribe to is not available through the iTunes Store, you can still subscribe to and listen to it using iTunes. Simply open the Advanced menu in iTunes, choose Subscribe to Podcast, type the podcast's Internet address in the dialog box that appears, and click OK. To locate podcasts that are not offered through the iTunes Store, try visiting a podcast directory such as podcastalley.com.

Regardless of whether you subscribe to a podcast from within the iTunes Store or from the Advanced menu in iTunes, episodes of that podcast are downloaded automatically to your computer. You can then listen to them at your leisure using iTunes.

If you want, you can specify how many new episodes should be downloaded automatically,

how frequently iTunes should check for new episodes, and which episodes are saved by default. To do so, click Podcasts in the source list and click the Settings button at the bottom of the screen. You can also download episodes of the podcast that were released before you established your subscription.

① In the Source list, click Podcasts.

iTunes displays a list of podcasts for which you have downloaded episodes.

② Click the arrow (▶) next to a podcast.

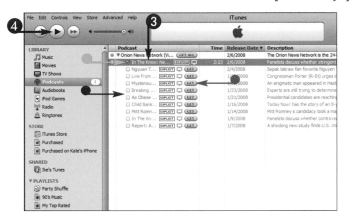

iTunes displays a list of available episodes (▶ changes to a ▼).

● Episodes that have been downloaded are indicated with a check mark.

● Episodes that are available but that have not been downloaded appear grayed out.

● To download a grayed-out episode, click Get.

③ Click the episode you want to hear.

④ Click the Play button.

iTunes plays back the episode.

Did You Know?

If you encounter any problems with a podcast that you have downloaded from iTunes, click the Report a Concern link below the list of podcast episodes in your iTunes window. iTunes directs you to a special page in the iTunes Store, enabling you to specify what type of problem you encountered (choices include Offensive Content, Difficulty Playing Episode, and Incorrect Category) and to type additional comments.

Listen to an Internet Broadcast

You can access hundreds of Internet radio stations through iTunes. Station formats include 50s/60s Pop, 70s/80s Pop, Alternative, Ambient, Blues, Classic Rock, Classical, Country, Eclectic, Electronic, Folk, Hip Hop/Rap, International, Jazz, Latino, Pop, Public, Reggae, Religious, Rock, and Talk/Spoken Word.

Although iTunes does offer direct access to hundreds of Internet radio stations in nearly

two dozen genres, there are thousands more Internet radio stations and other types of live streaming feeds — including live-broadcast concerts and sporting events — available online.

If you know the URL of the Web site that is broadcasting the Internet radio station, concert, sporting event, or other content, and if you are connected to the Internet, you can use iTunes to listen to the stream.

LISTEN TO INTERNET RADIO ON ITUNES

① Click Radio in the Source list.

iTunes displays a list of radio station genres.

② Click the arrow (▶) to the left of the desired radio genre.

iTunes displays a list of stations in the selected genre.

③ Double-click a station to listen to it.

CONNECT TO AN INTERNET BROADCAST

❶ Click Advanced.

❷ Click Open Stream.

The Open Stream dialog box opens.

❸ Type the URL of the site that hosts the broadcast you want to hear.

❹ Click OK.

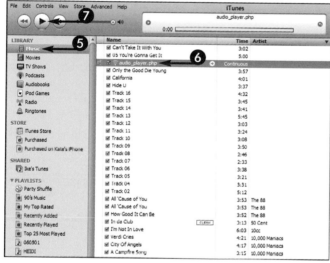

❺ Click Music in the source list.

An entry appears in your Music File list for the site that is broadcasting the stream.

❻ Click the entry in the file list for the stream.

❼ Click the Play button.

Important!

Unlike music and podcasts that you download from the iTunes Store and on your computer, Internet radio is streamed to your computer. As a result, you cannot stop or pause playback of a station; much like "regular" radio, whatever the station is playing at a given moment is what you hear.

Since its launch in 2005, YouTube, a video-sharing Web site that enables users to upload, view, and share video clips, has grown to host more than 70,000,000 clips, with an estimated 65,000 more added every 24 hours. Videos range from amateur-produced clips to content by major networks.

As great as it is to have so much content available to you, it does mean that finding a particular video can be akin to finding the proverbial needle in the proverbial haystack. Fortunately, YouTube provides various tools to help you find the video you seek. For example, you can search for videos by entering a keyword in the site's Search field, or else browse for videos by clicking various links.

① To direct your browser to YouTube's Web site, type **www.youtube.com** in the address bar.

YouTube's site appears in your browser.

② Type a keyword or phrase in the Search field.

● If necessary, click the (▼) and choose Videos.

③ Click Search.

● YouTube displays a list of links to videos that match the keyword or phrase you typed.

④ Click a video's link to view it.

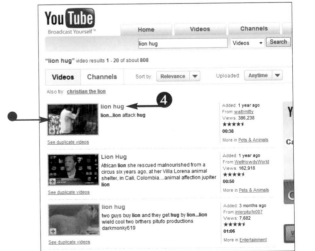

YouTube plays back the video.

More Options!

The sheer volume of content on YouTube can make it difficult to find videos of interest. For this reason, the YouTube staff reviews some videos, placing ones it deems interesting in the site's Featured Videos category, available from the site's main page. Simply click a featured video's link to view it.

Add a Video to Your YouTube Favorites

If you find a video you like, you can add it to your YouTube favorites. Then, anytime you visit the site, you need not search for the video to watch it again; you can simply select it from your list of favorites.

In order to mark a video as a favorite, you must first create a YouTube account. To do so, click the Sign Up link in the upper-right corner of the page and follow the on-screen prompts.

To remove a video from your list of favorites, click the Remove Video button under the video's entry in the favorites list. (To access the list, click the Account button, click Videos, Favorites, and Playlists, and then click My Favorites.)

---

① Click the Favorite link under the video you want to save as a favorite.

- YouTube indicates that the video has been added to your favorites.

② To view your favorites, click the Account link.

- Alternatively, you can view your favorites by clicking the Favorites link, if it appears.

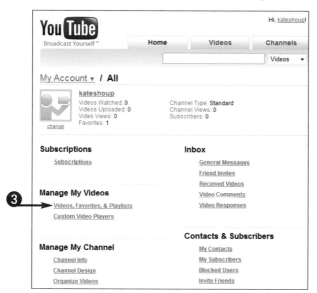

The My Account screen opens.

③ Click Videos, Favorites, and Playlists.

④ Click My Favorites.

● A list of videos you have saved as favorites appears.

Try This!

If you encounter a video on YouTube that you want to share with others, click the Share link under the video. Then, in the screen that appears, enter the recipient's e-mail address and, optionally, a brief message about the video. Finally, click Send Message. When your recipient receives the message, he or she can simply click a link in it to view the video.

If you have a video stored on your computer that you want to make available for viewing on YouTube, you can easily upload it to the site — assuming it is under 10 minutes in length and in any of the following video file formats: WMV, MOV, MPG, or AVI.

After you upload your video, you can view it anytime by clicking the Account button,

clicking Videos, Favorites, and Playlists, and then clicking My Videos. To remove the video from YouTube, click the Remove button that appears beneath it in the My Videos list.

Note that you must not upload copyrighted videos (unless, of course, you hold the copyright) unless you receive permission to do so.

---

① Click Upload in the upper-right corner of any YouTube window.

The Video Upload page appears.

② Type a title for your video.

③ Type a description.

④ Click the Video Category ▼ and choose a category.

⑤ Type some keywords, or tags, that people might use when searching for your video.

● Optionally, set broadcast, date and map, and sharing options. For more information, click each section's Choose Options link.

⑥ Click Upload a Video.

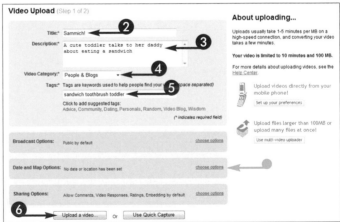

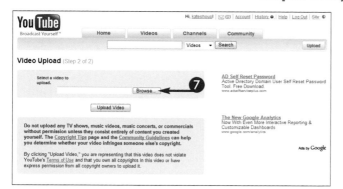

⑦ Click Browse.

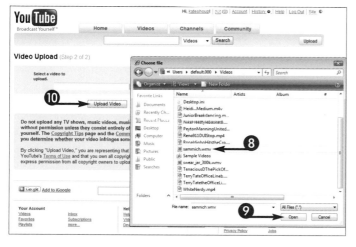

A Choose File dialog box opens.

⑧ Locate and click the video file you want to upload.

⑨ Click Open.

⑩ Click Upload Video.

YouTube uploads the video.

More Options!

If your video is larger than 100MB, or if you want to upload multiple videos, you can use a special program called the YouTube Uploader (assuming your video is less than 1GB in size). To install the Uploader, click the Use Multi-Video Uploader button on the right side of the Upload Video page and follow the on-screen prompts. For more information about using the Uploader, see YouTube's Help page.

Index

Index

Index

U

uniform resource locator (URL), 2
updating iTunes, 213
uploading
    photos to Flickr, 104–105
    photos to MySpace, 164–165
    videos to YouTube, 236–237
URL (uniform resource locator), 2

V

video
    adding to Blogger posts, 86–87
    adding to blogs with Blogger, 79
    adding to YouTube favorites, 234–235
    locating on YouTube, 232–233
    uploading to YouTube, 236–237
viewing
    photos in Flickr, 110–111, 128–129
    RSS feeds, 72–73

W

watching eBay items, 188–189
Web browser. *See also* security
    adding address bar, 14–15
    and blogs, 72–73
    browsing multiple pages, 20–21
    changing text size, 18–19
    customizing toolbar, 12–13
    default home page, 4–5
    favorites, 6–9
    Full Screen mode, 16–17
    history list, 10–11
    overview, 2

    performance, 24–29
    Skype button, 157
Web site
    foreign-language, 54–55
    phishing, 30–31
Web-based e-mail, 132
Web-based upload tool, Flickr, 104–105
Webcam, 155
Wi-Fi network, 46–47
wildcard character, 51
Windows Defender, 26–27
Windows Firewall, 40–43
Windows Live Hotmail. *See* Hotmail
Windows Live ID, 142
Windows Live Messenger. *See* Live Messenger
Windows Media file format, 86
Windows Photo Gallery, 204–205
Windows taskbar, 14–15
wink, Live Messenger, 147
worm, 40

Y

Yahoo! account, 102
Yahoo! Mail, 150–153
YouTube
    adding videos to Blogger posts, 86–87
    adding videos to favorites, 234–235
    locate videos on, 232–233
    overview, 210
    uploading videos to, 236–237

Z

zooming text in Internet Explorer, 19

Read Less–Learn More®

There's a Visual book for every learning level...

Simplified

The place to start if you're new to computers. Full color.

- Computers
- Creating Web Pages
- Mac OS
- Office
- Windows

Teach Yourself VISUALLY™

Get beginning to intermediate-level training in a variety of topics. Full color.

- Access
- Bridge
- Chess
- Computers
- Crocheting
- Digital Photography
- Dog training
- Dreamweaver
- Excel
- Flash
- Golf
- Guitar
- Handspinning
- HTML
- Jewelry Making & Beading
- Knitting
- Mac OS
- Office
- Photoshop
- Photoshop Elements
- Piano
- Poker
- PowerPoint
- Quilting
- Scrapbooking
- Sewing
- Windows
- Wireless Networking
- Word

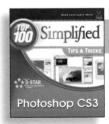

Top 100 Simplified Tips & Tricks

Tips and techniques to take your skills beyond the basics. Full color.

- Digital Photography
- eBay
- Excel
- Google
- Internet
- Mac OS
- Office
- Photoshop
- Photoshop Elements
- PowerPoint
- Windows